I0797516

W
WWW
W

WWW Drawing:
Architectural Drawing from Pencil to Pixel

Preface

Mehrdad Hadighi

There has been much recent conversation about drawing, perhaps due to the ubiquity of digitally-output 'drawings'. Articles have been written about the implicit value of hand drawing in comparison to computer-generated drawing; conferences and symposia on drawing have been held, even asking if drawing is dead!

WWW Drawing refers to two realms. One is the realm of the three 'W' authors – West, Wines and Webb – who came to the Pennsylvania State University's Department of Architecture in late March 2013, making large-scale drawings with students in the Stuckeman Family Building. The other is the realm of the World Wide Web. This pairing is intended to instigate an exploration of the realm of drawing in relationship to techniques and technologies, above all through the physical act of drawing, but also by thinking, theorizing and writing about it.

Drawing is always already a mediated task: by the eye, the hand, the mind and the instrument of drawing. The eye-mind-hand triangle – supposedly an unmediated, pure, environment for the passage of ideas, lines, and images – is far from that. At least since Henri Bergson's ***Matter and Memory*** (1911), we have known that the relationship between the world, its image on the retina, and our mental comprehension of that world is a mediated realm, far from pure, and far from direct. Following this logic, the eye-mind-hand realm is also a mediated environment. In this realm, techniques and technologies are only the most visible and outwardly expressed part of that mediation.

In fact, it is impossible to identify a 'pure', unmediated form of drawing, even in pre-'technological' times. The Ancient Egyptians invented and utilized a Wooden Corner Ruler, both for measuring and for drawing straight lines. The Nuragic people of Sardinia used compasses to draw circles. The Greeks invented a scaled ruler and used it to make architectural drawings. More complex drawing machines were invented more recently: Leonardo da Vinci invented a lathe-like machine in the late Fifteenth Century for drawing elliptic sections and, around the same period, Albrecht Dürer invented mechanical devices for drawing curves. In 1603, Christoph Scheiner invented the Pantograph to copy and scale drawings.

Drawing has been entangled with technique and technology since its inception, particularly drawings made for imitation. The Aristotelian definition of drawing as an imitative art placed it squarely in service of a referent – in Aristotle's case, of nature, the ultimate referent. In order to progress in this imitative arena, in representing the appearance of nature, questions of technique have always been paramount, and have not only assisted in depicting appearances; most importantly, they have shaped our cultural conceptions of our world, and our practices. Drawings of Chinese Gardens depicting depth as layers not only described their appearance, but also defined the Chinese Garden conceptually. The Renaissance invention of perspective as a drawing technique is intertwined with the Renaissance conception of 'man' as well as the Renaissance organization of buildings and public spaces. In the Twentieth Century, the use of cinematographic technique in drawing has also served as a conceptual tool for reformulating our understanding of reality and nature.

So, why now, with the invention of digital technology, do we ask if drawing is dead? Was it not dead, already, when we discovered one-point perspective?

What appears to be an altogether 'natural' drawing instrument, the pencil, was in fact not invented until the Sixteenth Century, when sheep farmers found a large deposit of graphite in England and used it for marking sheep, long before it was used for making drawings.

To restate: drawing is a mediated discipline. Its value is not constituted by how 'pure' it is, how it depicts, or how it expresses. Rather, its value is gauged in terms of critical practice: how drawing establishes and maintains a circulation between ideation and materialization, between things intelligible and things sensible. Although drawing appears as a static thing recorded on a medium, circulation is important in its conception. This is indeed the very thing that defines it. Every great drawing must circulate between the physical activity (whether by pencil, or by keyboard) and its criticism – the latter providing reflection that results in iteration and, thus, once again, a circulation through ideation and materialization.

Introduction

Janet Abrams

What is the role of drawing for architecture, in a digital age? What, if any, is the continuing relevance of drawing by hand, and how might computer drawing be inflected, in a positive way, by the errors and ambiguities of the hand?

In 2012-13, Pennsylvania State University's Stuckeman School of Architecture and Landscape Architecture conducted a multi-faceted inquiry into these rich and provocative questions. WWW Drawing was initially conceived, by Architecture Department head Mehrdad Hadighi, as a way to celebrate the 80th birthday of Professor James Wines for whom hand drawing has always been a crucial step in the architectural design process. Within its title, however, were implications of the digital technology that has become increasingly dominant within contemporary architectural practice. WWW Drawing would evolve to include several younger exponents of digital drawing, from within and beyond the disciplinary boundaries of architecture.

When I joined the Stuckeman School as Director of Special Projects for the 2012-13 academic year, the project had just two components, both earmarked for Spring 2013: a lecture series featuring Wines and fellow architects Michael Webb and Mark West (the Three W's) all renowned for their drawing techniques; and a giant-scale drawing workshop, with sections led by each 'W'. For the latter, Penn State architecture students would be momentarily unshackled from their keyboards and computer screens, and encouraged to luxuriate in the textures, gestures, physical expansiveness, and sheer filthy mess of making huge collaborative drawings by hand, using charcoal, oil pastels and graphite.

Shortly before the Winter break, an opportunity arose to mount an exhibition in the school gallery. By late January 2013, an exhibition of wall-sized and smaller drawings by the W's was in place – original works in ink, pastel, graphite and multi-media collage – providing the students direct access to work by their prospective tutors for the upcoming workshop.

I knew from experience that the process and outcomes of 'live' creative projects are often hard to predict and hard to convey through still images and captions. So I proposed we also make a video documentary of the WWW Drawing workshop. With departmental approval, we hired director Jane Nisselson, of Virtual Beauty New York, and her long-time collaborator, director of photography Rachel Strickland, with whom I'd worked on documentaries of multi-day live events produced by the University of Minnesota Design Institute. Together, we scouted the Stuckeman School building for promising sightlines, camera angles, and spaces propitious for the three different workshops, whose briefs were still under discussion. But it was already clear that each 'W' would require a different kind of environment, and would have their students using a range of drawing tools, equipment, and surfaces.

In many ways, the documentary makers helped us focus the workshops, not just visually (as subjects for the camera) but also architecturally, enabling us to determine which of the Stuckeman's spaces would work best for which workshop. The airy double height space, surrounded by balconies, at the center of the design studios, would be perfect for James Wines' assignment, in which his students would draw an 'expanding universe' in radiating sectors on a giant sheet of paper, rolled out on the floor. The stairs rising from third to fourth floor would allow Michael Webb's group to engage in an 'Exquisite Corpse' drawing game. And the penumbra of the single-story ground floor lecture/crit space would suit Mark West's workshop, where slide projectors would be regularly switched on and off, allowing individual students to trace fragments of the projected images then develop them into a dream-like overall composition.

In her essay, Nisselson describes the directorial strategy she developed to record activities that would evolve simultaneously, over two and half days, all over the Stuckeman building. She and Strickland approached the workshop through the lens and microphone, capturing the choreographies, rhythms and characteristic sounds of the various drawing processes as they unfolded. Their documentary reveals how each team of students adopted self-defined or assigned rules that eventually yielded three giant drawings, on a wall (West team), on a floor (Wines team) and up a flight of steps (Webb team):
http://www.vimeo.com/65680324

Given the connotations of the acronym WWW, it seemed crucial to include the perspectives of a younger generation of artists and architects adept at both manual and digital drawing technologies, who could speak to their advantages and shortcomings for contemporary architectural production. So the WWW Drawing project culminated with an off-campus symposium held at the Drawing Center, New York, in May 2013: presentations by Penn State University faculty members and artists and architects from further afield (Seattle, New York, Zürich) were followed by a roundtable discussion with the Three W's.

Architect Andrew Heumann had caught our eye with his spirited response to architect Michael Graves' ***New York Times*** op-ed article "Architecture and the Lost Art of Drawing" in which he unpacks the latter's arguments for the superiority of hand-drawing over computer drawing.[1] At the symposium, Heumann proposed that, rather than working exclusively in one or the other realm, contemporary architects tend to move back and forth between digital and analog. He identified questions that could lead to more productive hybrids: "What does manual drawing do ***better*** than the digital?" "Why are trace and pencil still so prevalent?"

1 Andrew Heumann, "Michael Graves, Digital Visionary: What Digital Design Practice Can Learn From Drawing," October 25, 2012 (http://acadia.org/features/H76XXP). Michael Graves, "Architecture and the Lost Art of Drawing," *New York Times*, September 1, 2012 (http://www.nytimes.com/2012/09/02/opinion/sunday/architecture-and-the-lost-art-of-drawing.html)

and "How can the digital better express imprecision, looseness, and ambiguity?"

Through his work as an architectural educator, design historian and curator, Daniel Cardoso Llach investigates the intersection of design and computation. In his essay, he underlines the core argument of his book, ***Builders of the Vision: Software and the Imagination of Design*** (Routledge, 2015) and identifies two distinct lineages of computer drawing: the "Algorithmic Aesthetics Tradition" versus the "Algorithmic Tectonics Tradition." He traces these, respectively, to aesthetic philosophers and computer drawing pioneers in the US and Europe, and to post-WWII scientists and engineers pursuing US Air Force-funded research at MIT. The fundamental difference between computer-made drawings and hand drawings, Cardoso Llach argues, is that the former have an underlying structure "encoded in the non-pictorial language of computers." Quoting CAD pioneer Ivan Sutherland (in whose memorable phrase, hand drawings are "only dirty marks on paper"), he shows how the de-coupling of image and structure in computer graphics is "not an opinion, nor a theoretical construct, nor a value judgment" but rather a practical distinction loaded with historical and cultural significance for architecture and other design fields.

Dirty marks on paper are certainly ***not*** how one would describe the drawings of artist Seher Shah, which have been exhibited at the Drawing Center and many other international venues. In her symposium paper, Shah describes her multi-city upbringing and its influence on her perception of architectural space, and her transition from training and working as an architect, to her current studio practice in which iconic works of modernism, such as Le Corbusier's Unité d'Habitation and London's Barbican Estate, are often the starting points for drawings, prints and sculptures. Through diverse media, Shah explores fundamental ideas about place, time and geography; the differences between public and private space; utopian city plans and idealized modernist architecture; and historical monuments and spectacles. Her work is characterized by sparse abstraction, economy of line, plays on geometry and perspective, and deep engagement in both the materiality of form making (whether 2D or 3D) and in the fundamental questions of social organization underlying architecture and urbanism.

Artist Ann Tarantino holds a joint appointment in Penn State's Stuckeman School's Landscape Architecture department and in its School of Visual Arts. In her talk, she credits two major experiences as having influenced her move "off the page...and directly onto the gallery walls." During a period spent working at the Drawing Center (long before this symposium) she came to appreciate the diversity of possible approaches to 'drawing.' Two years in Japan studying woodblock prints led her to the realization that "things could be simultaneously flat and spatial." Tarantino now uses drawing as a means of investigating space and responding to a given architectural environment, using various mark-making tools – from air compressors to laser cutters. The latter technology produces works that "lie at the intersection of hand and machine." When mounted directly onto windows, the resulting 'drawings' become animated by the light passing through their apertures, and cast corresponding shadows on the floors, yielding three-dimensional volumes from a two-dimensional surface.

Jürg Lehni describes himself as pursuing 'crop rotation' between arts, design and technology. Trained in engineering, interaction design, and media art, his work (usually made in collaboration with engineers, artists and graphic designers) takes the form of platforms and scenarios for production. In his paper, Lehni talks about his pursuit of gesture and poetic expression in the development of his software-controlled drawing machines, *Hektor, Rita* and *Viktor* – as well as his earlier 'software parodies' that critique the role of commercial design software in the creative process. Lehni thinks of technology as "a vocabulary and language that gives us the freedom to formulate processes and structures." As objects, his drawing machines are collages of industrial and manufactured components, physical counterparts to the modular character of software itself. But they also appear to have a life of their own once they're in motion, and actively drawing – a Frankenstein quality that Lehni amply conveys in his essay.

During the symposium round-table, a lively discussion ensued between the younger generation presenters and the senior W's whose papers are presented at the start of this volume. James Wines argues that the essential virtue of hand-drawing lies in its expression of an architect's visual 'signature' and situates this concept within a historical survey of drawing – from the Caves of Lascaux to the work of his own practice, SITE. In prose bordering on the erotic, Mark West conveys the lubricious tactility of drawing, as microns of carbon (graphite) are moved across a paper surface; he describes his method of making large-scale drawings (demonstrated in WWW Drawing workshop) as akin to "seeing shapes in clouds." And in an interview conducted expressly for this volume, Michael Webb surveys his decades-long experience teaching drawing to architecture students (at the Cooper Union and Pratt Institute, among other schools), explains his aversion to using digital technology, and argues for the crucial role of drawing as a method of critical thinking – of abiding value in the training of architects.

Since the WWW Drawing project, several conferences[2] have taken place on the role of drawing in architecture, in the US and Europe, examining both practical and theoretical aspects of the transition from the hand to the computer in conceptualizing, visualizing and rendering works of architecture. The present volume offers the viewpoints of a range of architects and artists from different generations, as a contribution to the ongoing dialogue on the relationship between hand drawing and digital technologies, and the processes of mediation and representation involved in making contemporary architecture.

2 Recent conferences on architectural drawing include: *Is Drawing Dead?* at Yale University School of Architecture, 2012; *Drawing Futures* at the Bartlett School of Architecture, London, 2016; *Between Paper and Pixels: Transmedial Traffic in Architectural Drawing*, TU Delft and Het Nieuwe Instituut, Rotterdam, 2016; *The Tools of the Architect*, European Art History Network conference, held at TU Delft and Het Nieuwe Instituut, Rotterdam, 2017; *Drawing Millions of Plans*, KADK, Denmark, November 2017; *Mastery and Uncertainty: the Drawings of Architecture*, Disegno 2018 at University of Louvain, 2018. *My Brain is in My Inkstand: Drawing as Thinking and Process*, an exhibition held at the Cranbrook Art Museum in 2013, featured work by a wide range of artists and designers.

The Three W's

Perspectives on a Life in Drawing

Michael Webb

Janet Abrams: Michael, You've been drawing for decades now.

Michael Webb: Seven and a half decades, if you count those done when I was six or seven years old.

JA: Do you 'do' or 'make' a drawing?

MW: That's a very important question. To 'make' a drawing implies a certain inventing, whereas a Working Drawing, where everything has already been designed (or so you delude yourself), would be a drawing you 'did'. But a drawing you 'make' has the implication of creativity. In French, there is presumably no difference: the verb ***faire*** translates as 'to do or to make'.

JA: How do you decide what to draw?

MW: Long ago, I developed a list of subjects I considered worthy of exploring through the act of drawing: a Drive-in House; a temporary environment of dwellings that would come and go; an elegiac study of a landscape that is dear to me. More often than not, my first stab at a drawing – derived from contemplation of the subject – would be disappointing, but a new drawing would grow, phoenix-like, out of its ashes. A drawing often starts out prosaic, even dull, but by keeping going, ideas as to its furtherance begin to present themselves. It can be years before I realize how a particular drawing should have been done. The process is self-perpetuating: the wretched shortcomings of a given drawing are expiated by its successor which, in turn, yields yet another new drawing.

JA: You trained as an architect in London at the (then) Regent Street Poly. How did that compare with your experiences as a member of Archigram?

MW: Polar extremes. The education I received at the Poly was very serious, well thought-out, but rather puritanical: all hard-edged rectangles, no frivolity – in keeping with the tenor of architecture at the time. So it was a bit of a culture shock to join these ne'er-do-wells producing this wonderful, exotic, erotic architecture. In early Archigram, especially from the hands of Ron [Herron] and Peter [Cook], one was supposed to ***enjoy*** making a drawing: beautiful colors were appropriate and desirable, as were photos of people having a good time inside the building. At the Poly, if you wanted to put a figure in a drawing, you should only show one and it should be there purely to indicate scale. In certain Archigram drawings, the figures occupied almost three-quarters of the drawing and you really had to look for the architecture behind them. **(Fig 1)** Which, if you could find it, was quite standard for the period: the space-frame roof truss, which Konrad Wachsmann had developed, and geodesic spheres, which of course Bucky Fuller started. None of us in Archigram were 'form givers'. The drawings weren't so much about the architecture, but rather the effect on social engagement that the architecture produced.

Ron Herron © Archigram Architects, *Batiment Public, Monte Carlo: Hendrix Interior.* 1969. Black ink line drawing, color film and newsprint collage. 36 cm x 28 cm

Fun fact: when the drawings were made, the beautiful young people were cut out from color magazines, then coated

2 Michael Webb © Archigram, *Three-Phase Horizontal Section through the Drive-in House*, 1995. Color-aid paper and airbrush (digitally corrected). 55 cm x 16.3 cm

Phase 1:
The car enters through an intake tube positioned vertically on the page. The white vertical line denotes the driver's center of vision. A convention of architectural projection drawing is that the plan of the building should be placed on the sheet (or screen) so the main entrance lies along its bottom edge; thus you can imagine yourself walking through the building's interior spaces by tilting your eyes upward towards the top of the drawing.

Phase 2:
The drum bearing the car has rotated clockwise so that its interior is now sealed off from cold air in the intake tube. Nevertheless, in order to follow the convention, the driver's center of vision remains vertical hence the rotating drum is graphically inert, while the inert house rotates graphically around the drum. (Slavish adherence to the rules of projection drawing thereby results in chaos in terms of readability.) The car doors begin to open.

Phase 3:
The drum has rotated further so the car now shares the same space as the schematic living area. Graphically, however, its position is such that the driver's steadfast center of vision is yet vertical. The car's doors are now fully open. As the car rotates about the house so does the sun (denoted by the yellow line in each phase).

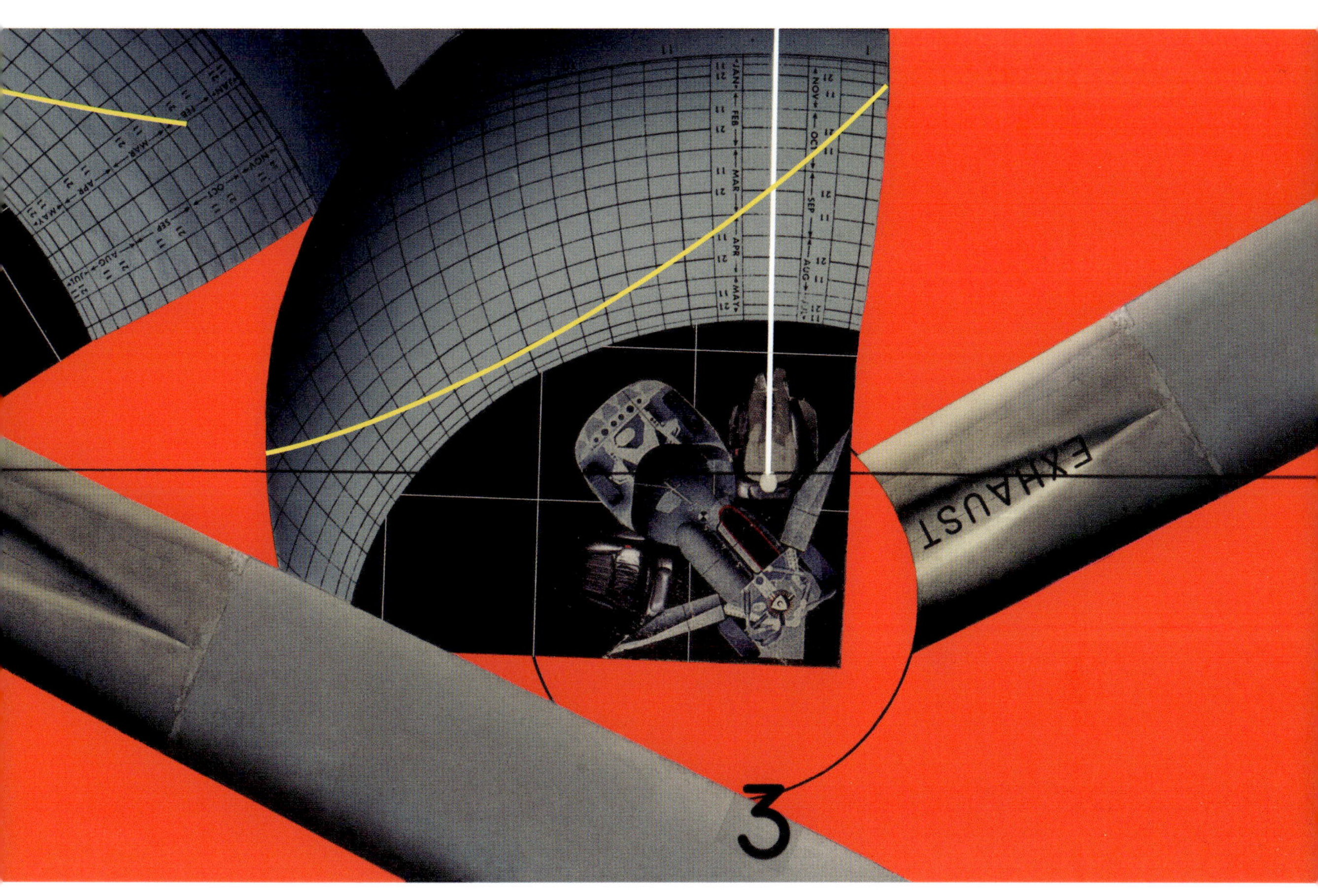
JAN FEB MAR APR MAY
NOV OCT SEP AUG
EXHAUST
3

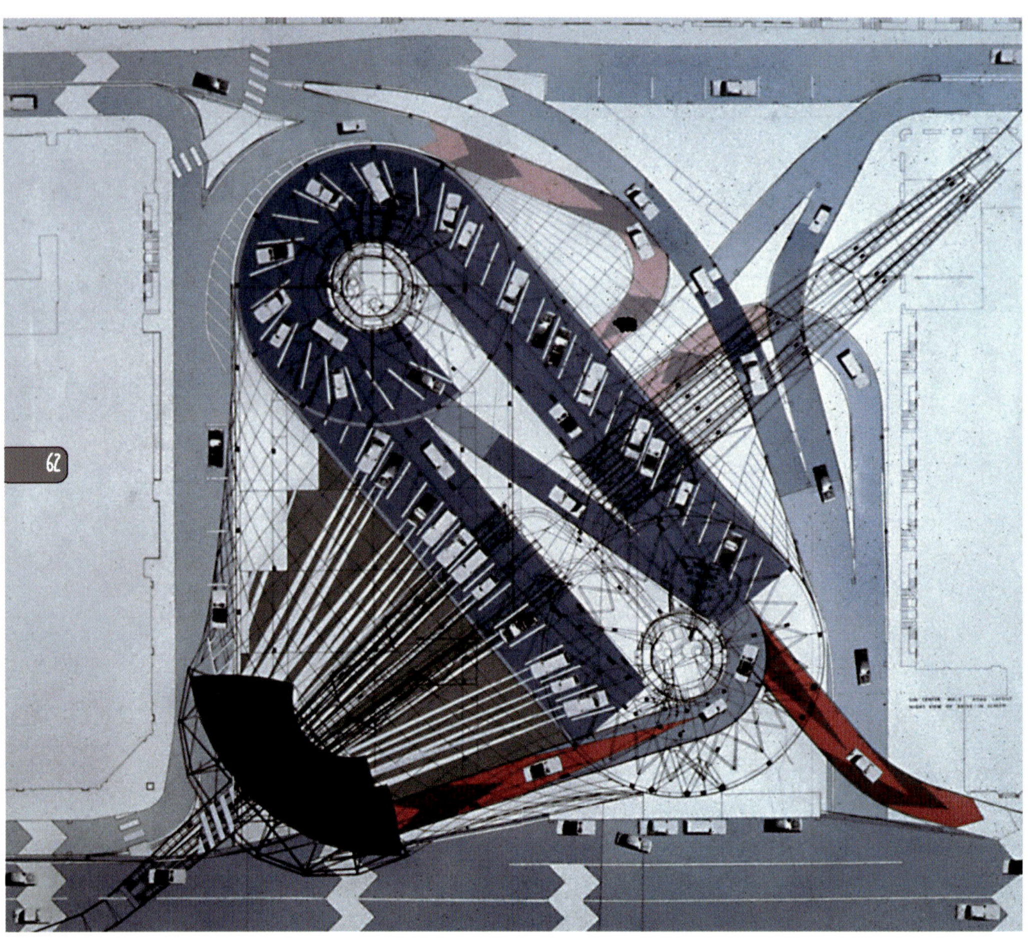

3 Michael Webb © Archigram, *Plan projection of the Sin Palace with added drive-in movie screen*, 1970.
Photographs of cars, colored overlays, and ink line on Mylar.
100 cm x 85 cm

with rubber cement to apply them to the surface of the drawing; they had perfectly clear skin, but over the years, it no doubt became blotchy. Same with the drawings: the rubber cement has started to come through the photographs, and they now look somewhat jaundiced, curling up at the edges!

JA: Sounds like *Dorian Gray* in reverse. Much of Archigram's exuberance came from looking across the Atlantic at the USA, right?

MW: During that time in London in the Sixties when we producing those drawings, the initial push was from the USA, but then England started to get cheerier and happier. The Mini car was an icon of cool young people with drive, as it were, and ambition.

JA: Since the Archigram period, you've moved on to making more 'romantic' images like the Temple Island Project, which you've been working on for many years. (Figs. 4-9)

MW: You use the word 'Romantic' because some of the later work reminds you of paintings by Turner, Claude Lorrain, John Martin. I wonder if the Archigram period isn't romantic also. It has very much to do with life and enjoyment, and maybe recollection and sadness...just a different way of showing it.

JA: True, in Archigram there's the romantic fantasy of a futuristic technological lifestyle projected via collage.

MW: You can't go on producing Archigram drawings forever. Each period of drawing you feel you've worked it to death. You need to move on, into a different realm.

JA: Your more recent work is incredibly painstaking – you lavish time and hand-skills on representation, in oils, watercolor and other media. I remember you steadily working on one painting from the Temple Island Project during your term as a 2011 Mellon Senior Fellow at the Canadian Centre for Architecture.

MW: In Montreal, I wanted to get involved in childhood recollection of the Henley Regatta, seeing where a study of the landscape would lead me. With the fear that it might only be of interest to me and my Mum. The Regatta course seemed potentially generative of numerous paintings and drawings: it's a textbook in basic perspective projection. All the rowing lanes are set out in the river, converging to a point on the horizon, virtually but not entirely covered by the temple on the island. The *Temple Island* drawing could be seen as a proposal for a giant structure, but one you have to *imagine*. There's an intimation that a building *might* be there, but in fact *is not* there. That's another way of being 'green'.

Cedric Price seems to me the ultimate 'green' architect: if he had the opportunity of *not* designing a building, he took it. Architects who fancy themselves as 'green' are still bent on making buildings; they just make them with sunscreens, active roofs and so on. But it's a much greater step *not to make a building at all.* If you cherish a landscape, you have to reject the invitation to impose a building on it.

4 Michael Webb © Archigram, *A cone of vision enclosing the landscape of the Regatta*, 1981. Watercolor on Schoellershammer Parole board, each board 75 cm x 50 cm

The image, composed of two adjacent drawings, shows only what an observer located at the apex of the cone of vision can see; he, she or they cannot see what is behind the objects of which the landscape is composed. These invisible components, therefore, are not shown.

5 Michael Webb © Archigram, *The temple dome projected onto a hemispherical picture plane,* 1978. Chinese ink wash on d'Arches paper. 50 cm x 37.5 cm

The beholder here is a floodlight casting a pool of light on a spherical surface – the dome of an aedicule, a temple whose dedicatee is supposedly Mother Thames. The floodlighting apparatus is attached by means of telescoping arms to a track set into the entablature of the drum that supports the dome.

As the floodlight circumnavigates the dome, it creates pools of light with continuously changing outlines. These shapes are then used as sectional profiles to create the form of the boat in which the Rev. Charles L. Dodgson, accompanied by the Rev. Robinson Duckworth and the sisters Liddell, will glide down the Thames all in the golden afternoon* – to quote the opening poem from *Alice in Wonderland*:

All in the golden afternoon
Full leisurely we glide

6 Above: Michael Webb
© Archigram, *The landscape of the Henley Regatta represented via a dot matrix*, 1987-2020. Oil on prepared board. 72 cm x 71 cm

The colors comprising the matrix are merely identical repeats of those found in the Munsell Color Sphere but in differing juxtapositions; so the painting can be defined as the colors found in the Sphere, multiplied and rearranged to create the illusion of an 18th century landscape painting.

7 Left: the Munsell color system. developed by Albert H. Munsell in the early 20th Century, specifies three properties of color: hue, value and chroma.

8 Opposite: Michael Webb
© Archigram, *The landscape of the Henley Regatta as a space/time image*, 2000-2020
Oil on prepared board.
110 cm x 45 cm

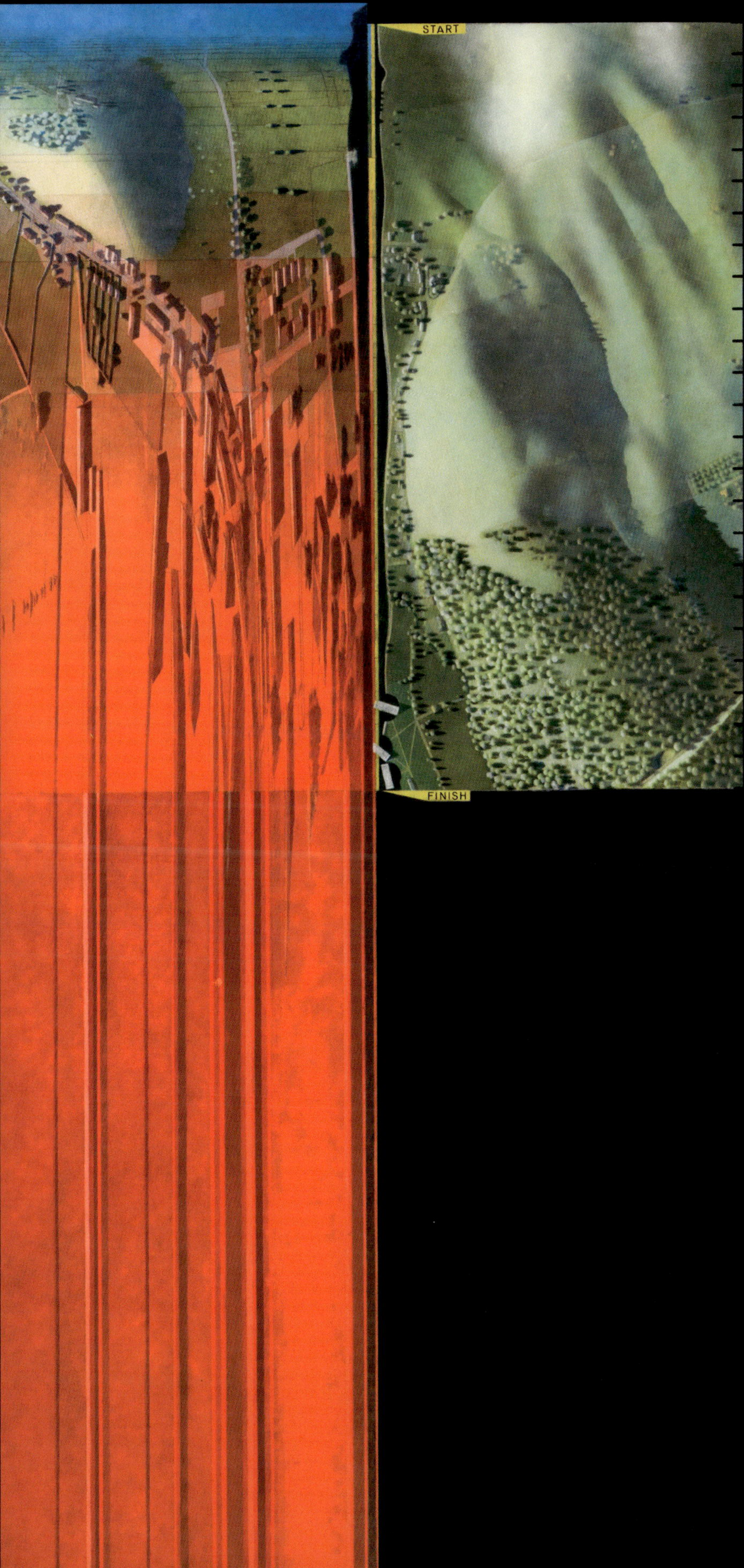
START
FINISH

9 Michael Webb © Archigram, *The landscape of the regatta viewed by a second observer whose viewpoint is located elsewhere* 2010-present. Oil on prepared board. 100 cm x 95 cm

I have moved my easel, as it were, from the apex of the cone of vision to another location; it matters not where. In so doing, voids have opened up behind objects in the landscape that are visible to all except the beholder standing at the apex of the cone. The planar truncation of the cone, whose surface is described by a hyperbola, means that these voids will erupt through it. For example, the void caused by the large weeping willow near the apex of the cone where it erupts through the surface, will reproduce at larger scale the outline of the tree's hanging tendrils.

A second willow, bottom left, further from the beholder, will record an outline where the increase in scale is less. It is assumed that the particulate matter in the air is at such a high level that the cone can be removed from the surrounding landscape as if it were a solid and examined independently, like an ice core. As soon as the beholder moves, the voids will start gyrating like movie gala searchlights and creating new gashes in the surface of the cone.

10 L. Ashwell Wood, *North-South vertical section through Grand Central Station*. Date of execution and size of original unknown. Airbrush and ink wash.

JA: **Common to all your drawings is an interest in perspective and games with geometry and optics. Can you summarize the core of your investigation?**

MW: I'm making some effort to understand the impact of a journey to infinity – what that would involve. Every perspective projection is a representation of infinity. When you draw infinity, you get a great mass of lines around the vanishing point, which connects to the idea of a black hole. My work is a geometric investigation that involves motion too: there's one drawing that shows a single point traveling towards the vanishing point at a constant rate.

The interesting thing about perspective projection – which supposedly presents objects as they appear in life – is that *it doesn't*. Drawing class professors warn students about the dangers of getting too close to the object they're drawing, because distortion may result! But it is just this distortion that interests me.

JA: **Tell me about the tools and materials you work with, and why.**

MW: For my oil paintings, I apply extremely thin, transparent layers of paint to the surface of a whiter-than-white commercially prepared board, with a 'tooth' just sufficient to hold the thin films of paint; any evidence of brush strokes is anathema to me! Rather than applying the paint with a conventional brush, I use a small piece of sponge attached to the handle of an X-Acto knife, dipped in the glaze and applied to the board. The colors of the paint appear richer when applied one on top of the other (and diluted with a blending medium) rather than mixed prior to application – for example, by applying a blue and an alizarin crimson to achieve a purple. Incoming light passes through the layers and is reflected off the white ground into the eye of the beholder. When combined with properly rendered shades and shadows, the painting seems to possess an 'inner light'. In this process – usually referred to as the glazing method – it's as if each layer of paint were on separate but superimposed sheets of glass. In that respect, it has a connection with color separation in photography.

I am moved by perfect gradients, and the astonishing light effects at sunset, especially when the air is heavily polluted. These I want to capture; no reason to ask why.

Lebbeus Woods once said to me that the two of us represented the wet and the dry. I wet, he dry. His medium was exclusively charcoal; he had learned how to apply unbelievably smooth gradients. Nevertheless, a close-up of his dark areas to my eye looks somehow rough. I preferred the smoothness in both close-ups and distance shots in drawings done with graphite pencil, where one starts with an 8H and works down to 2H, F and B. The problem is that you can't get a real deep black like with a charcoal drawing. So a graphite drawing tends to remain the shy, retiring type. If you use, say, a 2B pencil, the application tends to give off a rather unpleasant shine.

JA: **Why do you stick to hand drawing at a time when most architects have switched over to using computers for drawing?**

MW: There's a certain sensual pleasure, I must confess, in hand drawing. But that's not what's kept me at it. Rather, it's my total inability to understand digital technology. Hand drawing and painting require a skill level perhaps not fully appreciable by those who have wisely left the tools associated with our calling untouched. Sometimes, by sheer luck or intuition, the addition of a color or tone makes a drawing sing out: a joyous, albeit rare moment. In Proust's *À la Recherche du Temps Perdu*, the writer Monsieur Bergotte is amazed by a patch of bright yellow on a roof in Vermeer's *View of Delft* – a spontaneous gesture in paint, but so perfect that it must surely come only from God.

In *The Exquisite Corpse*[1], Michael Sorkin refers to the ballad of John Henry – the eponymous rail-spike driver who tries to beat the steam hammer at its own game – in describing the persistence of those architects who still draw by hand. *What do they think they're up to?* It seems to me that when one technology supplants another, the new doesn't eliminate the old, but makes it into something rarefied – something to be practiced with almost religious intensity. Like cooking.

1 Michael Sorkin, *The Exquisite Corpse: Writing on Buildings*, Verso Books, NY, 1994.

The availability of computer drawing doesn't mean the *end* of hand drawing, but puts it into a unique category: not dead but special in a way it never was before. With digital technology, so much of the image you produce isn't yours, but those who developed the program. When you open up Photoshop there's a long list of people who invented it. God bless them! How brilliant of them! So a drawing by Michael Webb is also by the people whose names appear on Photoshop's front page. With computer drawings, so much is given to you. Several semesters back I attended a review at an Ivy League school and the drawings were most disappointing: they all looked alike. In the days of hand drawing, those students who were intent on becoming architects really learned how to draw and usually did the good projects. The bad projects were badly drawn, though not always.

JA: You've taught drawing for decades. What do architecture students need to know about the history of drawing?

MW: Oh, *everything*. To understand computer graphics you need to know about the History of Drawing. Most drawing courses involve something being placed in front of you and you drawing it. I'm more interested in drawing where you have to *invent* the subject matter. That seems much closer to what architects do: conceive of something in the mind, reify it on a sheet of paper. Go into a Starbucks and there's an architect at another table – you can tell because he's wearing all black – talking to an associate. He pulls out a felt pen and starts drawing his latest creation on a napkin. The ability to represent what you have in your mind for your next building is *really miraculous*.

In a Drawing Class, you learn to do that such that the napkin drawing tells you where the design can go. If it's good, it can lead to the next stage of the design. If it's shitty, it won't do anything. Some students are quite inventive, intelligent, and dedicated, but nonetheless pretty poor at drawing. No matter what I say regarding hand drawing – that it's invaluable – some refuse to believe it.

JA: Give me some examples of your course assignments, and what you were trying to get the students to understand.

MW: I gave an assignment recently about putting the dining room from Buster Keaton's movie *The Scarecrow* on a two-dimensional sheet of paper. Everything on the table – marmalade, butter, plates, cups, salt, pepper – is hanging from strings, so if your partner asks for the salt, you just reach up, grab it and send it over with a pendulum-like movement. A drawing can represent very complex ideas but you have to limit its scope. *How do you interpret? What do you leave out? What do you* *include?* If you take some element of that meal, the drawing can handle it, but the elements still need to look like parts of a meal. Otherwise it's just a boring exercise in rearranging components.

In another assignment, I asked my students to think of Grand Central Station as a metaphor for the human circulatory system: the blood becomes people moving through the station. I showed them an amazing cross section drawing by L. Ashwell Wood **(Fig. 10)**, who drew for 1950s English children's comics, in which cutaway techniques are used to reveal what's hidden beneath the floor level and subway lines. *Revealing what can't be seen* is really important to consider.

I had them draw a very complex series of ramps beneath a pedestrian bridge. Then I showed them images of a semicircular rail tunnel no-one would know about unless they'd investigated the drawings, and asked them to place it on the drawing in its proper location vis à vis the ramps. Difficult because you're seeing not just what's in front of you, but also *what can only be conceived of.* The students came back with amazingly good drawings, pastels on dark colored paper.

JA: When you come across a student with the ability to conceive in three dimensions in their mind, what do you think that is?

MW: A gift from the gods. Like Mozart playing the piano at four. Somehow, it's born into them. What does *apotheosis* mean? *To lift up*? One student 'apotheosised' people as they crossed the floor of the main hall at Grand Central: their 3D forms became – not physically flattened – but 2D when they rose to the ceiling to take their place among the astrological figures, like Pisces, Gemini and Sagittarius. I thought it was a beautiful thing.

JA: *Apotheosis:* "The elevation of someone to divine status." Talking of apotheosis, have you sold any of your drawings over the last 20 years?

MW: No, no one's been interested in buying them; I've never done them on commission. It's only since the book[2] came out that there's interest in buying. And when you've been working on something for 25 years, it does make you think of asking a slightly higher price...

2 Michael Webb: *Two Journeys*, edited by Ashley Simone, with essays by Kenneth Frampton, Michael Sorkin, Mark Wigley and Lebbeus Woods. Lars Müller Publishers, 2018.

JA: Did you care about selling them?

MW: I didn't really think much about it. I knew they weren't ready to be sold. One chap who bought a painting, I asked him if I could have it back to do some more work on it. Still wasn't finished at the end of the month. He couldn't tell the difference, but it was quite clear to me...

JA: Is there something about not being able to let them go?

MW: Oh yes: avoiding disappointment. There's always the hope that with just a short amount of extra work, you will achieve a magical quality. Oil painting takes forever. But it's exactly that quality that appeals to me: you can apply a glaze of paint and if, the next day, you decide it was wrong, you can easily remove what you did with turpentine. Not much good for a student who has to finish her drawing in two days' time.

My dictum: *death is the only deadline.*

Found As in Clouds

Mark West

It is a common mistake, at least in academic circles, to believe that all meaning is produced and understood through symbols; that meaningful things are made in order to point to something else, something larger or deeper. *This stands for that.*

According to this semiotic regime, understanding a work of architecture requires a 'reading' of the work more or less equivalent to reading a kind of text – at its best, a poem of sorts. Meaning, in other words, is something you must *get.*

The semiotic basis of architectural meaning, while unassailable, is not our only means of communication or understanding. Music is a prime example of non-semiotic communication, in particular for the way its meaning arrives, beyond words or symbols, by surprise, and with the conviction of an irrefutable argument (while being nearly impossible to say, *in words,* what that meaning *is*).

In a CBC television interview from the 1950s I recently saw on YouTube, Vladimir Nabokov said about his novel *Lolita*:

> *I do not wish to touch hearts and I don't even want to affect minds very much. What I want to produce is really that little sob in the spine of the artist reader.*

Nabokov invokes the 'artist reader', making *us* the ones who find meaning by way of *that little sob in your spine.* (Did you even know you had a little sob in your spine?)

Loosely following in the spirit of Nabokov's invocation, I want to offer some examples of forms produced as a *secretion* rather than as a concoction or composition. Forms that arrive seemingly of their own volition do not have an intended meaning. (How can they, when their arrival is a surprise to their own 'author'?) Their meaning, if they have any at all, will only be received (*found, discovered*) after the fact, through involuntary reactions.

The following examples both pre-date and accompany my work with quasi-'self-forming' concrete structures. I urge you to keep in mind that these are not representations of anything. These are analogical things – theatres that play out through the illusion of images, a way of making in which authorship is relinquished in favor of phenomena.

On Form-Eruption Drawings

Graphite is the crystalline form of carbon, and is used industrially as a dry lubricant. But the lubricating qualities of graphite were dormant in the pencils I had been taught to use. Its wet and slippery nature was revealed only when the rigid and willful specificity of architectural drawing slipped and fell.

Cursory research reveals a few underlying qualities of graphite that are attuned with its lubricating and mutagenic potentials. Graphite is an allotrope of carbon (allotropy is a property held by certain chemicals that allows them to take two or more different forms, the other common form of carbon being diamond). Graphite is an electrical conductor that displays super-lubricity (a condition in which friction vanishes).

Carbon is, coincidentally, the chemical foundation of life as we know it. This has no bearing at all on drawing, but makes the substance itself a bit heavier in your hands. This potent combination of physical/mechanical properties conspires, under fortuitous conditions, to assist the discovery of unexpected and spontaneously emergent forms and images – a lubricated automatic 'writing' of sorts.

'Drawing' is a kind of pulling. Drawing with graphite amounts to pulling your hands through a lubricant. The feeling, when it is going right, is a bit like moving

1 Mark West, *Everything Falls*, 1983-86. 76.2 cm x 91.44 cm 'Blackout' drawing: graphite on paper photo collage.

grease around with your fingers, or modeling wet clay, although all this is taking place in an infra-thin space though microscopic, translucent, layers clinging to the minute surface landscape of the paper. This is all felt through the hand and fingers – a kind of remote sensing of the drawing paper's surface and the microscopic dry, greasy particles piling up and clinging to it.

The geometry of the graphite tool tip (the pencil's point) changes as it is drawn across the paper in the following ritual sequence: first a cone, then a truncated cone, then a chisel that sloppily erodes towards a ball-point, now too far gone.... then sharpened to a cone, and so forth.

These minute changes in the shape of the tool tip are 'seen' by feeling its special friction across the paper's surface. The difference between a sharp tip and a ball-shaped point is immediately felt, even though the altered geometry is barely visible to the naked eye. The shape of the point is seen through the sensors of the fingers. If you are attentive, the fingers enlarge the tool point, like a microscope, until the pencil tip is felt more like a bar of soap being drawn across a sidewalk's concrete surface. The graphite's microscopically fine grease is grabbed by the hilltops of the paper's surface through dark repetitions in this enlarged internal landscape. The mutual lubrication of paper, hand, and mind begins to pull the mind's eye through this same darkened landscape, causing a mutual lubrication of interior and exterior perspectives. Hand and eye, charged with this slippery darkness, slide along a surface landscape of emergent forms and images, pulling them across and through the paper's surface. It is a falling, where perfectly clear forms volunteer themselves to us, exactly as they do in clouds.

It is possible to make drawings by clarifying the forms that appear in the gray graphite clouds. Such a drawing produces a picture that is not a depiction, or at least not a depiction of anything that exists in the world outside the drawing. The forms that offer themselves, if they are clarified with sufficient gentleness and fidelity, present a vivid and compelling realism – though this sense of realism is attached to things ***that don't exist outside of the drawing's illusions.*** The vividness of the illusion, however, is a seduction towards the sense that these things ***could*** exist. These are not drawings that indicate or function through signs; it is quite a bit more like secretion or conjuring than representing.

Consider for a moment how odd it is to see things in clouds. However strange or contorted, these images are so perfectly formed, and their perception so effortlessly and spontaneously arrived at, that it appears that clouds actually form themselves into these shapes.

This is, of course, absurd. Clouds are ***not*** shaped like men's faces or whales, or horses' bodies, or any of the other myriad figures we see in them. They are only, and always, shaped like clouds. It is ***we*** who see these other figures in the cloud's own forms, produced in a kind of waking dream. Indeed, they won't appear at all without taking time to ***stare*** into them for a while.

In a form-eruption drawing, the fundamental act is one of dutiful and meticulous clarification of the images that spontaneously appear before one's eyes. This must be done gently with the lightest of strokes and the most sensitive spreading of the translucent graphite as tone and contrast is amplified and adjusted. Anything too brash, willful, or forward will collapse the game, and you will end up merely making marks on the paper indicating this or that, and the compelling 'realism' of the illusion will be lost. As the surface of the image one sees becomes gently clarified, it is simultaneously and necessarily altered into

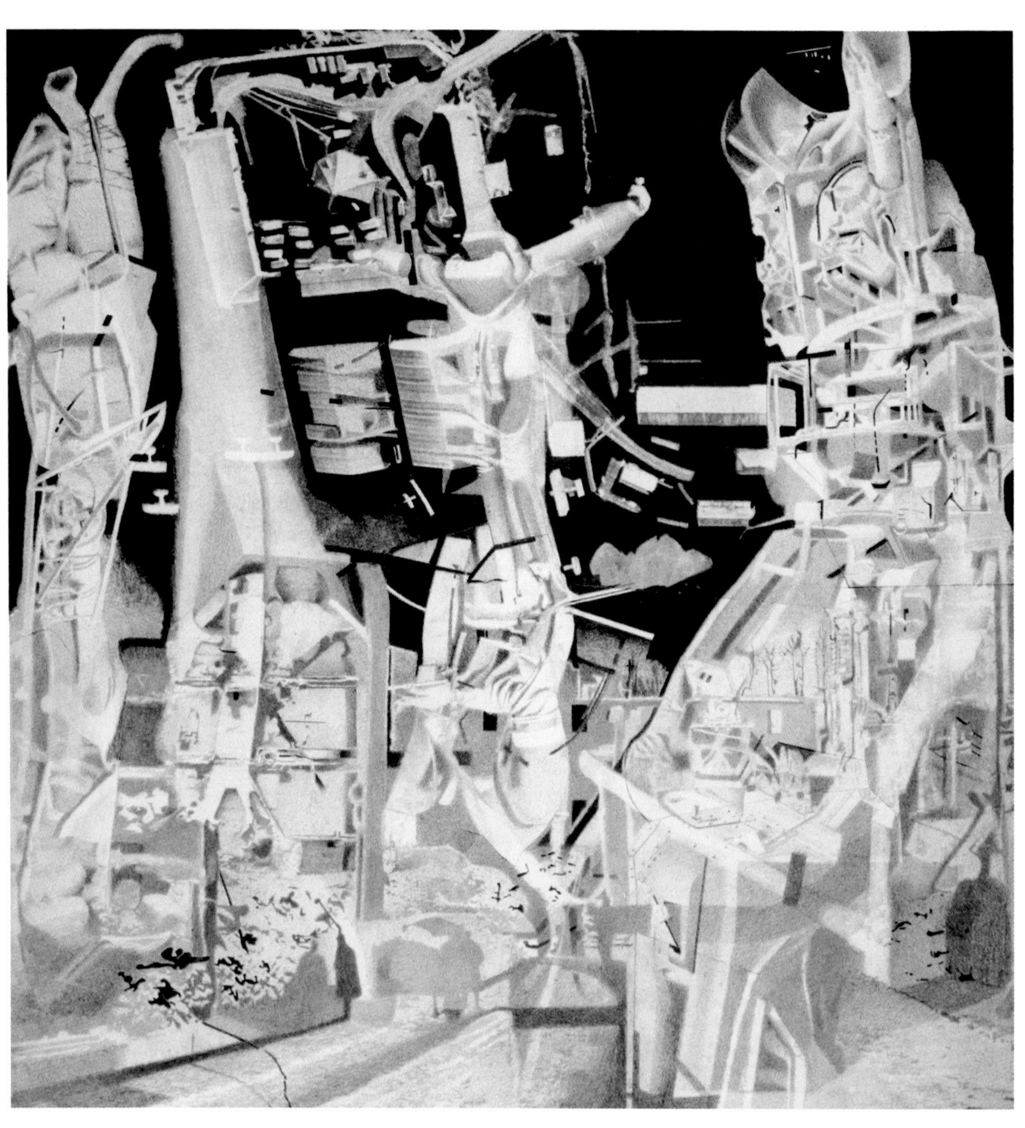

2 Mark West. *Welcome To The Neighborhood*, 1983-86. 'Blackout' drawing: graphite on paper.

Opposite page:
3, 4 Mark West. *Everything Falls*-details. 'Blackout' drawing: graphite on paper photo collage.

5 Mark West. *Welcome To The Neighborhood*–detail of photo collage.

its next mutation, obscuring the very image being clarified, and resolving into a new image according to its own altered terms. This new emerging image is itself clarified/altered, in a fluid game of an image chasing itself, destroying itself, to find an emerging new self.

A time-lapse film of such a drawing would show a slowly seething field of mutually emergent and altering forms, rolling, roiling towards the final image, which is chosen and fixed through nothing more than a timely suspension of action. In this way the final image both contains and obscures the many previous forms and images that constitute the morphogenesis of the picture. They are 'in there', yet no longer visible as themselves. The author of such a drawing – if we can use that word for someone who is only following what is already given to sight – holds a secret knowledge of the drawing's inside story. The drawing is felt, at least by its author, to be more alive because of its inner geology, its hidden layers and past incarnations.

On Collage Construction Drawing

A variant of form-eruption drawing – what might be called 'Collage Construction drawing' – provides a way of making test 'constructions' of spaces and buildings based on existing models and constructions. In such drawings, photographic fragments from various physical constructions are optically projected onto a sheet of paper and roughly assembled as a collage. Then they are drawn into being by both willful and hallucinatory techniques, as a way of finding and rendering a possible architectural reality. It is like using your hands and eyes as organs of imagination.

The selection of source material and its initial collaged arrangement sets the nature the game, which is played out in a series of improvisations that oscillate between the free-fall of form-eruption 'finding' and the willful invention and depiction of designed constructions. In this way, a dream-like freedom is maintained even as possible constructions are tested and architectural propositions are made.

The state of mind induced by this way of drawing is reminiscent of descriptions of lucid dreams in which a mixture of vivid and unexpected occurrences are guided by the author's active will. These more willfully constructed drawings can begin from collisions of disparate source materials, but they can also dream into a particular scene, exploring the architectural possibilities of a specific setting though hallucinatory suggestions and projected ideas of construction.

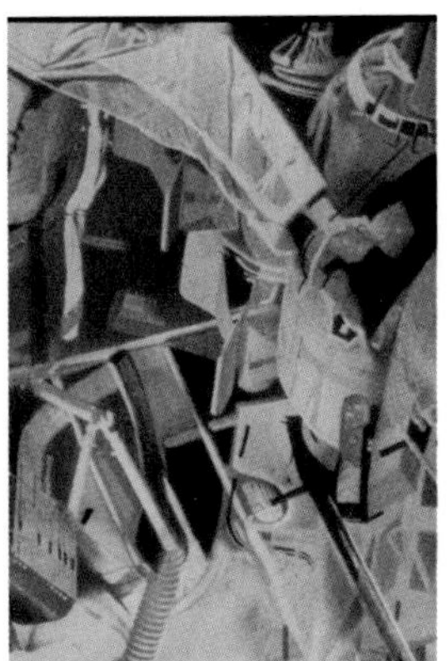

Color

The color drawings shown here are are made through essentially the same means as the graphite drawings, though their material basis is a bit different. The drawings start from photographs that are digitally collaged and then printed onto drawing paper (or canvas if you are painting). Colored pencils are used to draw inside and on top of the base collage image. The waxy dust of the colored pencils is selectively dissolved, here and there, by an application of turpentine, loaded onto a blending stub (those small paper cones traditionally used to spread and blend graphite or charcoal).

The ink of the printed base image sets the start of the drawing's chroma. The initial color decisions are, in this sense, pre-made before the actual drawing begins. They are simply a fact within the print, a site condition of the work. The colors, as they arrive, also produce a layer of chromatic links across the page: those yellow things; those pink things, and so forth, are automatically linked by color alone, regardless of their form or meaning. The affect afforded by color is felt like a soundtrack played over the illusion of form, providing a kind of polyphony accompanying the play of form, space, and light. New dimensions of sensual pleasure, not available in black and white, involuntarily arrive.

Compared to the monochromatic illusions of the graphite drawings, these colored dreams are somehow more reminiscent of life, or life-in-the-world. In a parallel way, the idea of a *mechanism* more easily gives way to that of *organism* when these dreams are bathed in color. This, in turn, suggests a project of similarly linking architecture itself more closely to life by turning attention away from its fixation on form.

6 Mark West. *Ancient City* – detail. Colored pencil on paper-printed photo collage.

7 Mark West. *Ancient City*, 2011.
50.8 cm x 50.8 cm
Colored pencil on paper-printed photo collage: a form-eruption drawing in color.

8 Mark West. *Construction* - detail. Coloured pencil on paper-printed photo collage.

9 Mark West. *Construction*, 2014.
58.42 cm x 53.34 cm
Coloured pencil on paper-printed photo collage: a form-eruption drawing in color.

10 Mark West. *Nebula*, 2017.
73.66 cm x 58.42 cm
Coloured pencil on paper-printed photo collage: a form-eruption drawing in color.

11 Mark West. *Lace Maker*, 2018.
73.66 cm x 58.42 cm
Coloured pencil on paper-printed photo collage: a form-eruption drawing in color.

A Line Around an Idea

James Wines

We should talk less and draw more. Personally I would like to renounce speech altogether, and like organic nature, communicate everything I have to say in sketches.
Johann Wolfgang von Goethe

It is often said that Leonardo drew so well because he knew about things; it is truer to say that he knew about things because he drew so well.
Kenneth Clark

Drawing is putting a line around an idea.
Henri Matisse

It may seem strange to champion hand drawing today, in view of the universal triumph of digital graphics. Every progressive architect in the world seems obsessed with elevating computerized delineation to new heights of illustrative supremacy. But while the software revolution has increasingly taken precedence, there appears to be a fresh incentive among many architectural students – a kind of quiet revolution – based on a new-found desire to hone their manual skills and learn to draw in the old way.

I have long been a supporter of dual skills, encouraging young designers to maintain equal graphic abilities on paper surfaces and computer desktops. It is my deeply felt conviction that by focusing exclusively on computer generated illustration, something conceptually profound is forfeited in the design process. When electronic response mechanisms replace the filtration of idea development through tactile means and guiding fingertips, the fertile territory of 'subliminal accident' is lost. I'm referring to the marginal calligraphy that dribbles off the edge of the paper, the inadvertent congestion of squiggly lines with no apparent meaning, the unwelcome blobs of ink that drop off a pen tip, or the inclusion of seemingly irrelevant references that have nothing to do with initial intentions. Many times over the years, I've been the creative beneficiary of my own graphic musings – of the chaotic trail of ambiguous images left behind by random charcoal smudges and watercolor washes. In a variety of miraculous ways this pictorial detritus, hand drawn on paper without any pre-determined architectonic mission, has often become the springboard for new ideas.

Frequently, when watching some youthful computer whiz use software to whip out multi-dimensional views of a complex structure in a matter of minutes, I feel I may be pushing a hopelessly old fashioned aesthetic ritual, as a consequence of some deep-seated psychological resistance to the cybernetic world.

A decade ago, when proficiency in computer rendering was being applauded as some kind of transcendental feat, I recall how impressed I was with the photo-fidelity of digital drawing. Everything churned out in those days looked too good to be true... and it was. As my eyes became accustomed to sifting slickness from substance, I gradually acquired an aptitude for detecting mediocrity (or outright crap) lurking under the pictorial gloss. To the point where I can now spot digital dazzle camouflaging conceptual vacuity at fifty feet from the screen.

One advantage the computer can never offer is the kind of calligraphic proficiency needed to draw really well. As I frequently explain to architectural students, this elevated status is a combination of aesthetic instinct and responsive rendition that goes considerably beyond the conventional ability to produce photo-like images with great fidelity – a commonplace talent in architecture, frequently mistaken for genuine drawing.

Mechanical reportage also forms the basis of computer graphics and is the primary reason that digital tools will always be best employed as an efficient means of confirmation (describing the big idea after it has been conceived), but never a deeply resonant art experience in itself. When teaching drawing to young designers, their most noticeable deficit is a lack of understanding of the complex aesthetic challenges in accomplished draftsmanship. These include knowledge of the origins of language, the evolution of calligraphy, the nature of signification and the abstract dimension that unites positive and negative visual elements on the picture plane. I am still speaking mainly of drawing in its subsidiary role as a means of recording one's thought process within the larger goal of building design. But, as in an artist's study for a painting or sculpture, the calligraphic quality of the initial sketch is always a determining factor in its ultimate qualification as an aesthetic experience.

Among architecture students, the tradition of illustrative purpose often seems to hinder their grasp of the 'deep structure' content of drawing, with its multiple layers of readings. For this reason, it is important – especially in the computer age – to understand the contributions of structuralism in language analysis to the broader understanding of both literature and art.

The discovery of the Altamira and Lascaux cave paintings (in 1879 and 1940 respectively) confirmed the fact that Paleolithic cultures as far back as 30,000 years ago had mastered the art of drawing and established the foundations for all subsequent graphic selection in the formation of written language. Contrary to the previous view that Cro-Magnon people were simply hunter/gatherers, a privileged and talented minority within these communities – perhaps designated religious shamans – were relieved from their foraging obligations. Given the consummate artistic quality of the cave murals, this level of mastery was probably the result of centuries of stylistic refinement: nothing with this level of aesthetic resolution could have occurred without a significant investment in both the urgency of communication and its translation into culturally-endorsed nuances of line, tone and color. The illustrative factor was certainly part of the purpose of cave art; but those Magdalenian painters also knew that the profundity of visual language resided in its abstract and iconographic elements – in the connections between inscription and philosophy.

Picasso reportedly wept when he first viewed the Spanish cave paintings, exclaiming "After Altamira, all is decadence." As one of the greatest draftsmen in history, he understood that these prophetic Neolithic artists had anticipated not only the development of Egyptian hieroglyphics and Chinese calligraphy thousands of years later, but also the ***signifier/signified*** basis of linguistics, and the role of mind and hand in the evolution of visual ideas. In referring to Magdalenian art as 'proto-writing.' historian Andrew Robinson seems to assume that Ice Age people did not yet have a legitimate language. But there are enough abstract symbols punctuating the cave murals to suggest that these Cro-Magnon painters had laid the groundwork for the development of written language, as well as all subsequent calligraphic innovation in art and design.

A remarkable stylistic consistency links the art of Lascaux and Altamira with other cave paintings in Chauvet and La Marche in France, as well as those found in Africa and Australia. For example, bison, deer and wild boar are represented with extraordinarily sensitivity in terms of linear and tonal choices – parallel to those skills found in the drawings of artists Da Vinci, Rembrandt, Van Gogh, Matisse and Giacometti, and architects Alberti, Piranesi and Wright.

In prehistoric times it was only a small aesthetic/linguistic leap to associate the gracefully tapered legs of a bison with all forms of stability and movement in nature. The next step was to abstract this anatomical fragment into a pictogram, refine it into a cuneiform inscription and, finally, amplify its meaning with phonetic markings and syllabary alphabets. By logical extension, this process evolved into the serviceability of e-mail on one hand and the expressive pathos of Picasso's Guernica drawings on the other.

There's a link between the deep sense of symbolism and lyrical representation in the depiction of hunted mammals in Magdalenian culture, and the advent of written language in Asia. Following a similar route 4,000 years ago, China had already developed calligraphy to the point where fragments of the first alphabet are still part of contemporary Chinese writing. This interface between language development and the aesthetics of drawing is at the core of graphic expression, which thrives on renewal and reinvention. As linguist Noam Chomsky describes it, "Language is a process of free creation; its laws and principles are fixed, but the manner in which the principles of generation are used is free and infinitely varied." Even the interpretation and use of words involves a process of free creation. To his "use of words" must be added the "use of line."

Chinese writing and drawing have remained synonymous skills in the hands of Asian calligraphers since the first pictographs emerged; in later dynasties, 'ideographs' were used to embody fully developed narratives. Like all languages, Chinese underwent a logical development from the faithful contour depiction of such images as 'man,' 'sun,' 'ox,' 'water,' etc, toward a more complex system of signs needed for phonetic/semantic functions. The continuing beauty of Chinese characters is their metamorphic quality – moving gracefully back and forth between representational and conceptual realms of signification. This "art of language" has kept Asian painters and poets continuously supplied with renewable source material and perpetuated the role of calligraphers – a true fusion of theater, communication and graphic style.

At the core of Chinese calligraphic aesthetic is the gestural rhythm of the pen or brush stroke, and manual control demonstrated by the flow of thick and thin lines. But it is the raggedness of edges, spontaneous splatters, and inadvertent drips, and their collective interaction with negative spaces that I consider to be the essential ingredients in the multi-layered practice of drawing. For the master Chinese calligrapher, these indeterminate factors are usually captured in bold gestures, but the same spontaneity and fragmentation can be manifested in the smallest lines on paper.

A number of my recent drawings explore the integration of architecture and landscape, often in situations where the building is located in a natural site and the objective is to preserve as many trees as possible. The resulting architecture appears to be consumed by its own environment or, more perversely, as a victim of "nature's revenge." Other renderings describe the need for more forested areas, water sources and urban agriculture in the cityscape; architecture and context are integrated to such a degree that it becomes hard to discern where the building ends and the environment begins. Vegetation, topography and climatic conditions become as much a part of the aesthetic fabric of a structure as masonry, glass and steel.

My architectural practice SITE, has developed a fluid interface between multi-media and conceptual development, as is clearly demonstrated in our project for "Residence Antilia" in Mumbai, India. Realized through a combination of hand

and digital drawing techniques, the calligraphic underpinnings of this proposal appear in multiple formats, scales and qualities of line, tone and color, through its various stages of representation – source referencing, search-for-idea sketches, design clarification and renderings made for pure aesthetic experience. Designed in 2003 for industrialist Mukesh Ambani, this residential tower is located on a very restrictive hilltop site, overlooking the city of Mumbai. In response to the client's desire for a multi-tiered, landscaped structure, similar to the ancient Hanging Gardens of Babylon, the entire building is conceived as a 'Vertiscape' garden in the sky, freeing park spaces from their normal earthbound confinement. This concept corresponds with Vastu principles in Hinduism, in which the spine is considered the main source of support, leading upward toward enlightenment. The residence's seven levels are supported by a heavily reinforced structural core, stabilized by steel cables that support five 'floating' floor planes and a variety of garden terraces, verandas, trellises, viewing platforms, water features and recreational facilities. All horizontal projections emerge from this core, similar to the role of vertebrae in the spine. In accordance with Chakra meanings in architecture, the building's various zones are linked to themes of earth, water, fire, air, sound, light and information. The main residence, on a crowning 4000 sq m platform, continues the unifying theme of stratification.

My advice to young architects seeking to draw in order to develop ideas (or for pure pleasure) is to follow Picasso's obsessive example: "I draw like other people bite their nails." In his enthusiasm for the power of the hand, the great Spanish artist purportedly took a dim view of the digital revolution, commenting: "Computers are useless. They can only give you answers." While reflecting a certain 1960's naiveté concerning the emergent computer age, Picasso nonetheless correctly prophesied the current revival of interest in hand drawing and the growing acknowledgement that there are conceptual and aesthetic territories that Form Z, AutoCAD and SketchUp software can neither equate, nor replace.

When I watch masses of architectural students locked onto computer monitors as if prosthetic extensions of their own bodies, and churning out facile simulations of buildings, I recall Baudrillard's eerie assessment of Post-modern culture, especially his views of media phenomena as illusions that are replacing reality.

In a world of simulacra, I find that signs scratched on paper with a pen or pencil have a way of restoring the authenticity of representation, as well as the validity, socially relevance and symbolic content of the object or place being described. As Baudrillard astutely observed, the illusions created by media tend to remove people from the organic and tactile world around them. Retaining this connection between mind and hand seems just as valid now as it was for the cave artists who immortalized the hunt in Lascaux and Altamira.

The quest for calligraphic quality is no less relevant – an objective perfectly captured by an anonymous quote I found recently on the Internet:

"We all have at least 100,000 bad drawings inside of us. The sooner we get them out and onto paper, the sooner we'll get to the good ones buried deep within."

James Wines, *La Ville Radieuse - La Biennale d'Architettura di Venezia*, poster for SITE project, 2000. Ink and wash.

James Wines, *Post Global Warming-Adaptive Re-use of Existing Buildings at Sea Level*, 2006. Pen, ink and wash.

James Wines, *Public Administration Town City Center-Seoul, Korea-Garden City Concept*, 2006. Pen, ink and wash.

James Wines, *Body Transformation*, based on Hong Kong. 2014. Ink and wash.

James Wines, *Highrise of Homes*. 1981. Ink, wash, and charcoal.

James Wines, *New World Plaza-Urban Forest-Beijing, China*, 2008. Pen and pencil.

James Wines, *Residence Antilia and 'Vertiscape' Park-Mumbai, India*, 2003-04. Ink, wash, and charcoal.

‘s

WWW Drawing Workshop

The WWW Drawing workshop took place over a weekend in March 2013. The Three W's each led a group of students in creating a large-scale drawing — using different materials and approaches — in three different spaces within the Stuckeman School of Architecture and Landscape Architecture.

This spread and next two spreads: Michael Webb's team creates a collaborative drawing by following a set of rules developed by the students, using charcoal and pastels on individual sheets of colored paper. In the eventual drawing, these sheets climb the stairs of their workspace, combined according to an Exquisite Corpse strategy.

YOU CAN ONLY
START AT THE INTER
SECTIONS OF LINES

You can only Draw
from Bottom to
Top (No back Tracks)
HAVE TO
IN
PERIPHERY

Webb group collaborative drawing being pieced together as an 'Exquisite Corpse'. Still from WWW Drawing workshop video produced by Virtual Beauty, New York.

Mark West's group works on a 'Collage Construction drawing' by tracing selected portions of photographic images, projected onto a wall-mounted horizontal sheet of paper. The digital projector is switched on and off intermittently, allowing the students to take stock of their individual graphite tracings, and to 'find forms as in clouds,' – eventually joining their separate drawings into a single collective image.

Center left: Mark West leading by example.

West team at work: each student traces over selected portions of digitally projected images.

James Wines' group develops an image of the Expanding Universe on giant sheets of paper, each taking responsibility for filling a segment of the circular drawing with their own imagery, in dense charcoal. The scale of the floor-mounted drawing surface requires full-body interaction, and careful movement across the accruing image — the students equip themselves with white socks and t-shirts for the occasion.

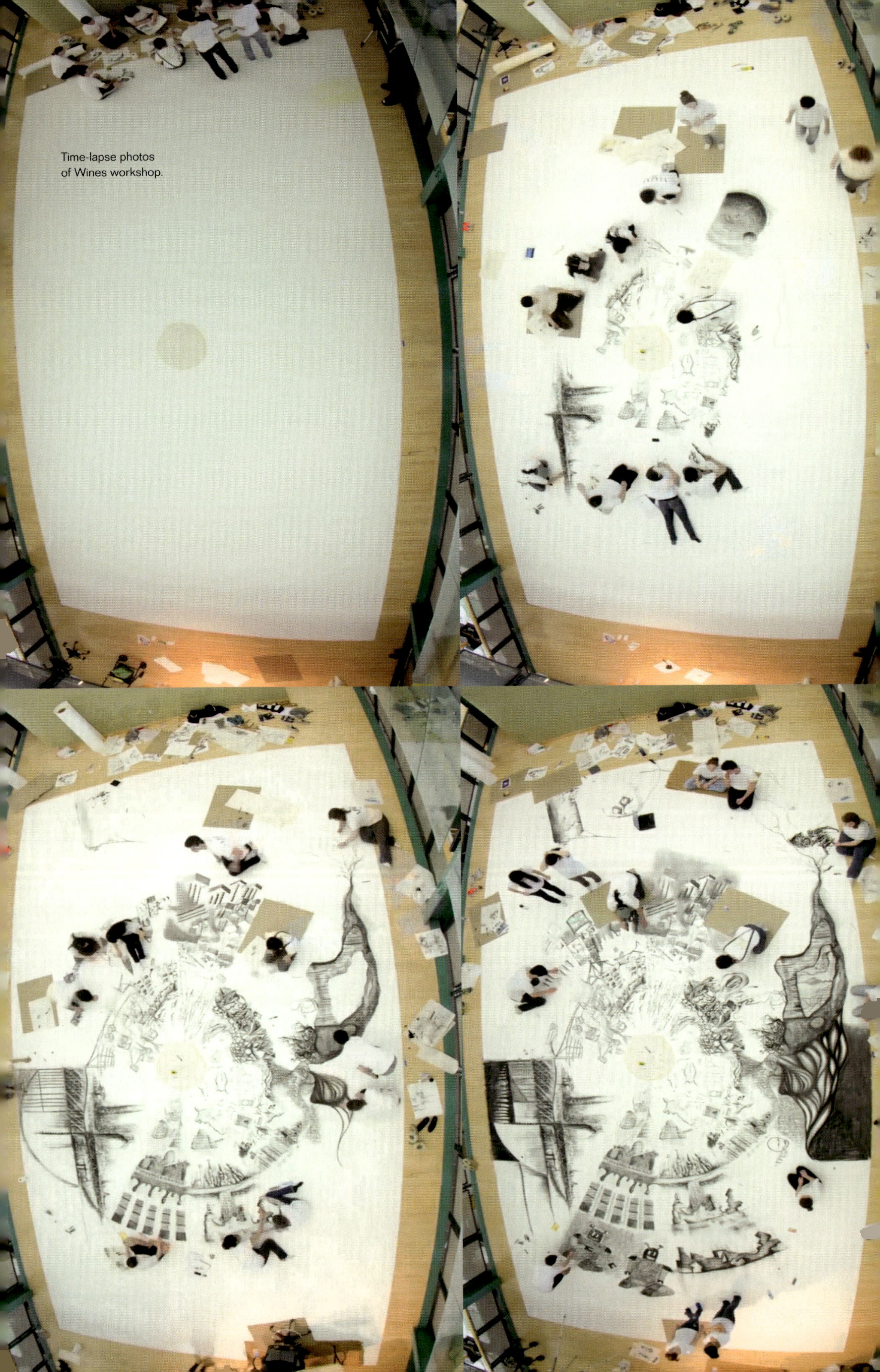

Time-lapse photos of Wines workshop.

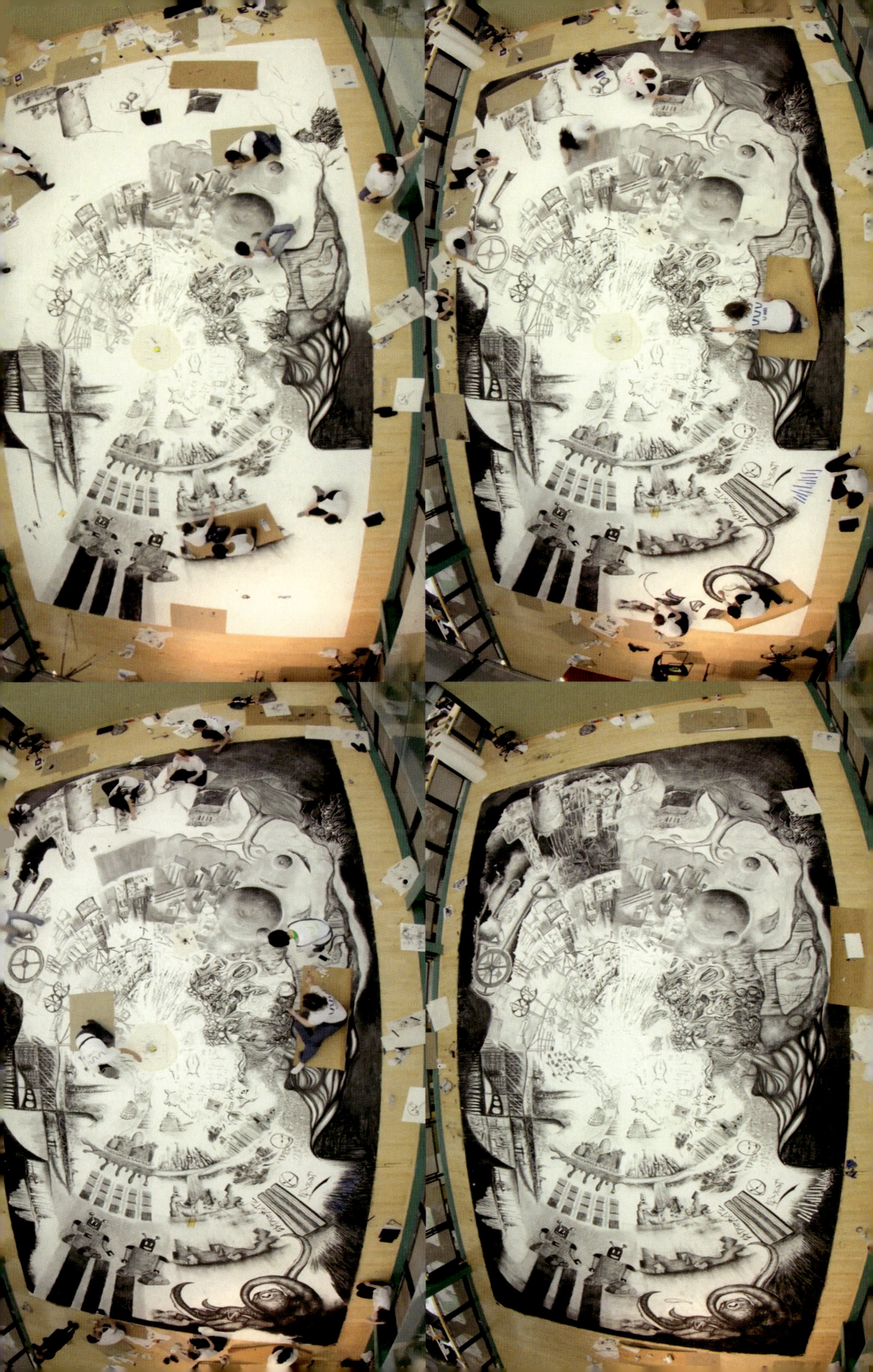

Drawing Through a Lens

Jane Nisselson

As filmmakers, we were immersed in a two and a half day drawing scrum. Our job was to capture three architects in three spaces, each directing a student group in the making of a large-scale drawing. The processes and final drawings couldn't have been more different and that was the wonder of the workshop.[1]

We also encountered an unanticipated X factor: drawing performed by groups. Master compositions emerged equally through personal expression and hands-on team collaboration.

In addition to wielding cameras amidst the drawing performance, filming logistics were shaped by the fact that each production took place at a different location in the architecture school building. As it turns out, the settings actually spatially organized the drawing processes, while they disorganized ours. One of our goals was forecasting where and when the action would be happening.

1 WWW Drawing Workshop video: http://www.vimeo.com/65680324

Recording Drawing
Hardware: lens

Cinematically, our wide shots portray drawing as clusters of people in a landscape of paper, charcoal, pencils. Mark West's group applied marks on a sheet of paper affixed to the wall. Their movement backward and forward in the room was pure choreography. Sketching on the floor plane, James Wines' group concentrated into huddles. Michael Webb's activity anarchically spread across wide steps that graduated upward from the third to the fourth floor. With a wide lens, you could see the whole drawing too.

It is in a medium shot that drawing manifests as a verb, a personal activity. The image is close enough to reveal the physical movement of the individual in contact with the drawing surface.

In close-up, the signature of drawing is actually the sound: stroking and tapping rhythms that indicate observation, timing, decisions.

Mark West
Assignment: Finding through Making
Film technique: dolly in, dolly out

Each mark is its own thing with its own voice and its own existence.

In many ways this workshop was about the intimacy of making a mark. We had to close in on the activity, with West in the midst, and caught dialogue as he coached a student to connect to the carbon. About a pencil, "It's an extremely sensitive tool because imagine what you are doing, you're moving things at a microscopic scale, you're moving atoms of material around."

The wall at one end served as a vertical drawing surface across which a wide sheet of paper hung. To jumpstart drawing, color photographic images were digitally projected as a collage onto the drawing surface, at various intervals in time. The students traced. The projectors turned off, the students moved to the back of the room to consider the work as a whole. Mark West, "Take some time, stare into the images and you start seeing things that could be there."

Drawing then resumed, lights on, as the group moved back to the paper to develop a composition unrelated to the initial images but inspired by the marks that had been made.

Projection on, projection off. Step forward, kneel, trace with a pencil, elaborate, take many steps back, lights on, sit or stand, discuss, lights off, march forward, bend or stand, move atoms, projection on. Repeat. Pure Merce Cunningham. This back and forth movement in space for perceptual shifts cued our shooting.

Our choreography included following the students detaching and rotating the drawing 180 degrees and then rehanging, upside down. According to West, "Interrogate the drawing by turning it upside down, your authorship is out the window."

Dolly in, dolly out.

Michael Webb
Assignment: Procedural Drawing
Film technique: crane

Freedom is the most terrible thing to ponder, and if you have a set of rules you can't break, life is much easier. That was the point of the rules.

Placing the drawing activity in a space that was a flight of Eisenstein-like Odessa Steps, Webb mutinied. This space subverted drawing – both process and the final composition. So the drawings were not flat. By the end, they weren't even rectangular. Unlike Wines' group who wandered, walked, sat and sketched exclusively in the horizontal space of their composition on the floor, the drafting surfaces for Webb's group were not fixed horizontally as one might expect on tabletop or floor. Nor was the working space vertical, pinned to the wall like West's. The angle flip-flopped up and down the six steps, with 2.5 feet tall rises and 5 foot runs.

All drawing employed a prescribed vocabulary stylistically derived Webb's Archigram drawings. Additionally, the students designed a set of 10 rules for executing the drawing process. Authorship was annihilated as students changed spaces (and drawings) at timed intervals, applying their own rule to each drawing, one at a time. Webb himself intervened in these drawing sequences with a bright orange piece of charcoal.

In the time lapse you can see all conceivable drawing positions: standing, leaning, kneeling, sitting, lounging. The horizontal plane of the step functioned as a table and the vertical side as an easel.

"Treat [the drawing] as a graphic, two-dimensional object" instructed Webb. The next bit of insurrection was that the drawings did not remain as rectangular compositions. Individual drawings were assembled into a master work that ran

up and down through the space of the stairs according to an Exquisite Corpse directive. "Even though it doesn't seem right" urged Webb.

So, we too zigzagged up and down, pivoting in 270 degree arcs to film the drawing activity, with the effect of a crane.

James Wines
Assignment: City as Expanding Universe
Film technique: zoom

All great drawing has somewhere under it what I would call the fingerprints of the idea.

Our cinematographer astutely placed herself in position to film a wall-to-wall roll of paper as it was unfurled across the space of a large, balcony rimmed, double height room. "The floor plane is the drawing, the theme is based on the expanding universe," James Wines explained. "The core center ... represents an intense billionth of a second when the big bang occurred which sent everything out into orbits around each other and out into space."

We captured a kind of human compass sketching this core and then, with spoke-like lines, dividing cosmic space into eight pizza-like wedges. Small teams executed their themed slices: natural, underwater, sinful, linguistic, bizarre, pleasantville, industrial, historic. Perhaps working from a verbal list, inherently abstract, led this group to primarily draw in a representational mode, verging on illustration.

In the famous Hans Namuth footage, Jackson Pollack confronts his floor bound canvases, leaning over or in a squat, "I feel nearer, a part of the painting." Here, Wines' students' universe was directly on the plane of paper. Gravity held for the most part. The teams worked their way out from the central vertex of their triangular lots, sitting, lying, leaning, often carefully placing themselves on pieces of paper, occasionally standing up for a break. iPads with reference images were scattered about.

One student equated the mechanics of his revolving stroke of a circle to the mechanical world he was sketching out. Representation did get bigger at the edges where the outer circumference and spokes disappeared, so perhaps the universe does expand.

Wines surveyed from on the balcony above, not quite in another solar system, directing, "Everyone should come up here once in a while, have you all been up here? Keep that expanding universe feeling".

We went up and down. Zoom in, Zoom out.

About our team:
As a documentary filmmaker, Rachel Strickland was as much co-director as cinematographer. Cody Goddard recorded the audio – absolutely essential to documentary and experiencing drawing. He also helped with just about everything else including lending and setting up (along with Eric Weiss) our time lapse cameras which revealed the patterns of making.

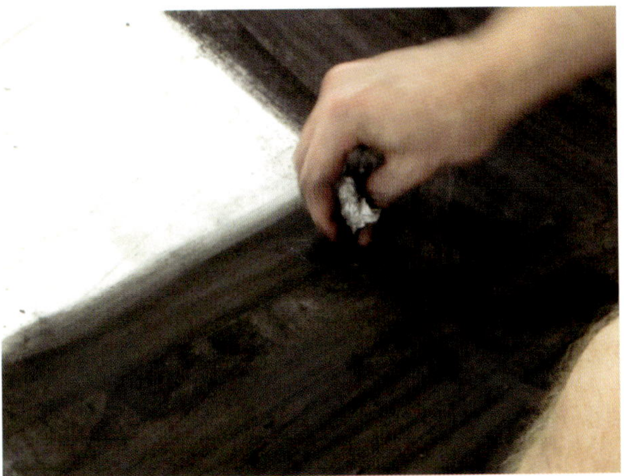

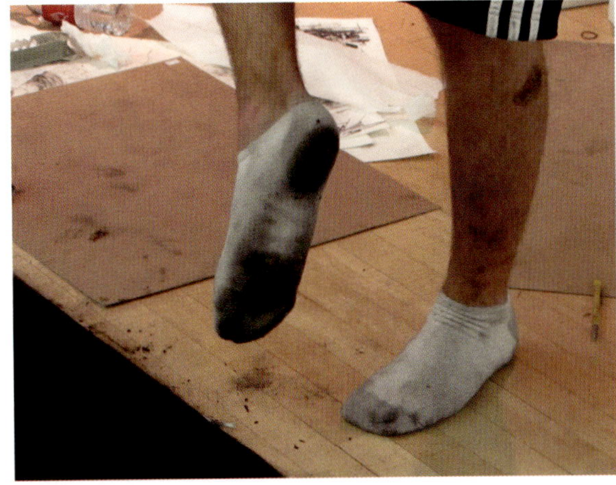

What Digital Design Practice Can Learn From Drawing

Andrew Heumann

I'm going to start off with a confession: ***I cannot draw for the life of me***, despite four years' worth of drawing classes in high school and college. I nearly quit architecture school in first year because we weren't allowed to use the computer in any capacity; everything was hand-sketching and hand-drawing. I only survived by cheating, primarily by modelling all my projects in SketchUp, printing them to scale, and then tracing by hand or on the drafting table – even adding construction lines so it looked like the drawings had been set up manually.

So I was relieved when, in second year, they finally let us loose on the computer Even this split – first year, second year – was representative of the disciplinary rift I sensed in my education, between old school and new school: hand-drawing and drafting versus scripting, rendering and modeling. There was a lot of pressure to situate yourself in one of these camps. Because I was rather awful at drawing but good at scripting, I felt like I'd fallen into the latter camp.

Michael Graves argued that the computer is great for technical drawing and precise final documents, but for anything with a creative capacity – anything that stimulates your imagination – the computer just doesn't cut it.[1]

1 Michael Graves, "Architecture and the Lost Art of Drawing," *New York Times*, September 1, 2012.

On the other hand, Patrik Schumacher, at Zaha Hadid's office, has written extensively about the disciplinary shift from drawing to scripting. He sets up a kind of progress narrative from hand-drawing to 2D CAD, to 3D CAD, culminating in associative parametric modelling, where each technique renders its previous incarnation obsolete.

Even though I associated myself more with the digital/scripting side at work, I wasn't really comfortable with either side of this debate: the rear guard felt too limited in its understanding of technology while the self-proclaimed avant-garde was trying to throw out everything else.

In reality, the way people actually practice usually discards this debate and works with productive hybrids. I recently saw a designer at my workplace tracing over her computer screen! We use the tools for what they're good at, and cycle back and forth.

In their 2008 book ***Opportunistic Architecture***[2], architects Lewis.Tsurumaki.Lewis describe this process really well, as an active moving exchange between scanners, printers, software, and parallel rules. They acknowledge the different capacities and tendencies of these tools, and permit their work to be inflected by each cycling. I think hybrids like these are a really productive way to work today, but they also reinforce the notion that drawing is one thing and the digital is another, and the only way to transgress that separation is to work between them.

2 Lewis.Tsurumaki.Lewis, *Opportunistic Architecture*, New York: Princeton Architectural Press, 2007.

As a digital practitioner, I'm interested in what drawing does *better* that the digital might learn from. Why are trace and pencil still so prevalent? What are the capacities of drawing and how might they be incorporated into digital practice? Are there fundamental limitations with the digital that prevent this from happening? Or might an evolution of software or hardware or practice allow some of these more creative and fluid tendencies to be inflected into digital practice?

The first aspect of digital practice with which many traditional practitioners take issue is the interface of the mouse and the keyboard. James Wines has written about this, talking about the importance of the fluidity of the connection between mind and hand, and how that determines the quality of the architect you become. He laments the way students get locked into computer monitors as prosthetic extensions of themselves.

This idea of the digital device as a prosthetic extension is quite interesting; it's possible to become *quite good* with a mouse and keyboard. Anyone who's actively working digitally internalizes the commands and holds them in muscle memory. There's been an evolution of interfaces towards stylus and gesture, and the capacity for haptic feedback – such that, when drawing with a stylus on a screen, you can sense the texture of the digital medium – offers many possibilities for future digital platforms. (Fig. 1) This is already in use for 2D digital drawing, but might get folded into 3D, as well.

Researchers at the Technical University of Munich have developed an interactive platform that uses foam cubes on a projected surface and an object that controls the viewpoint. (Fig. 2) You sketch over these objects and your sketches get projected back to the three-dimensional model. The platform can also sense

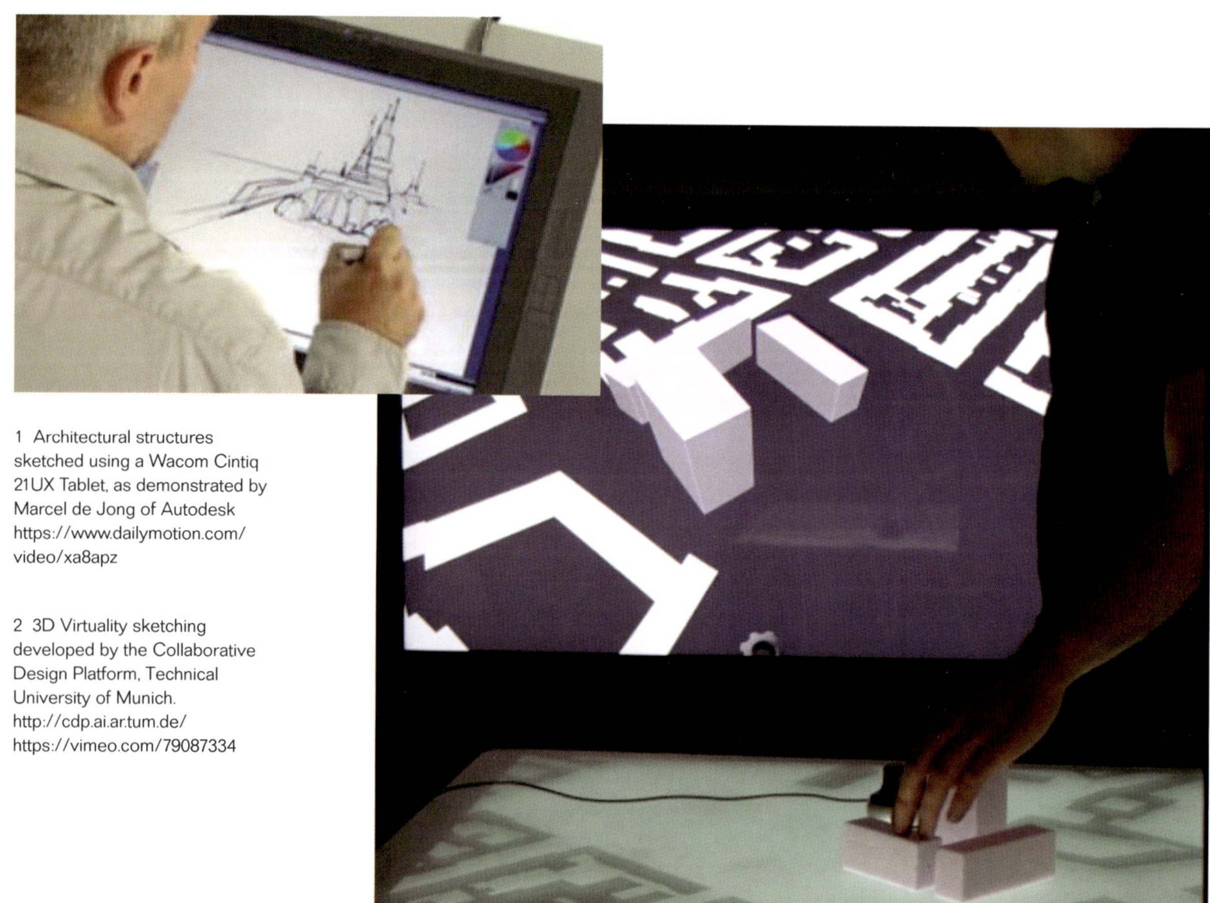

1 Architectural structures sketched using a Wacom Cintiq 21UX Tablet, as demonstrated by Marcel de Jong of Autodesk https://www.dailymotion.com/video/xa8apz

2 3D Virtuality sketching developed by the Collaborative Design Platform, Technical University of Munich. http://cdp.ai.ar.tum.de/ https://vimeo.com/79087334

the 3D geometry of the foam blocks. You can cut the block and the 3-dimensional transformation will occur on this system, as well. It cycles between a physical three-dimensionality and a 2D projection that layers over a flat piece of 'virtual' trace. A modelling platform like this holds a lot of promise, as a way of engaging all facets of your embodied cognition.

One of the advantages of hand-drawing is the ability to go out into the world and draw from life. A huge limitation of the digital, in this respect, is ***portability*** – which is a hardware issue. We don't tend to bring our laptops and 3D modelling platforms out into the world but, presumably, as devices get smaller and thinner and lighter, this will become possible. The issue is less about being out in the world than about this process of drawing from life using the same tool to ***record*** that you use to ***generate***.

In my last year at school, I took a parametric approach to this notion of modelling from life: I built parametric sketches of existing buildings – for example, the Eames House. **(Fig. 3)** Just as you learn about a building's internal organizing systems by doing a sketch of it, this way you're literally ***concretizing*** those systems. Even though it produced a reasonable representation of the Eames House, it was also capable of producing hybrids from exactly the same structured system.

Another widely-discussed aspect of hand-drawing is expressivity and the personal touch. The question is: how can one communicate ***imprecision*** and ***looseness*** through digital drawings that are always inherently precise. One approach to this is the sketchy look you see in a program like SketchUp. This is really just a filter lying on top of a 3D model. It doesn't really give you anything.

I've noticed that in academic practice, even in the last ten years, there's

3 Andrew Heumann, digital drawings from *Parametric Case Study* of the Eames House, 2012.

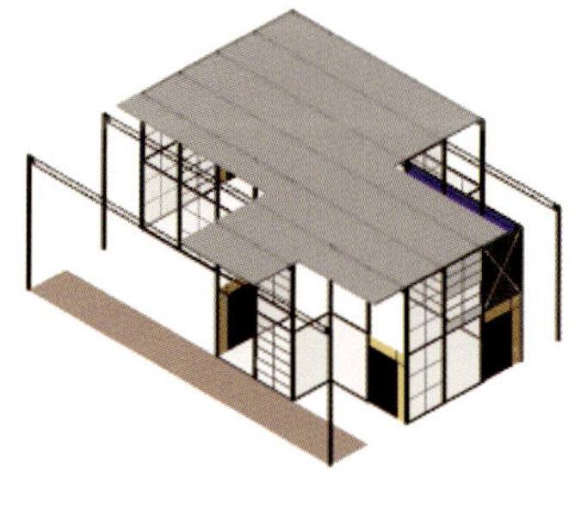
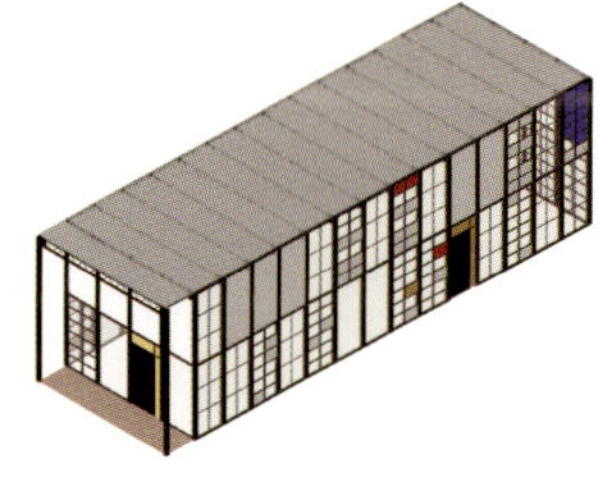
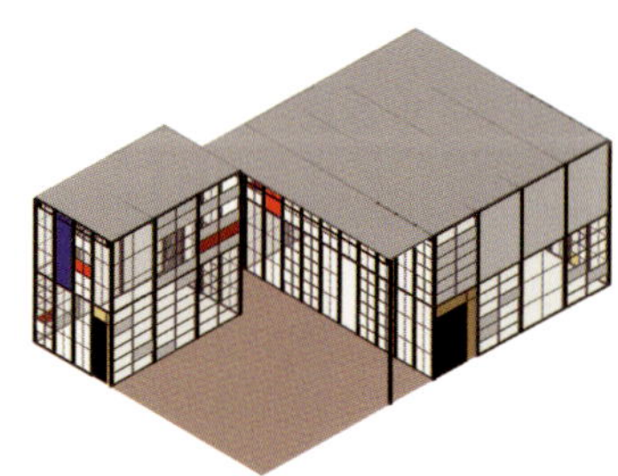
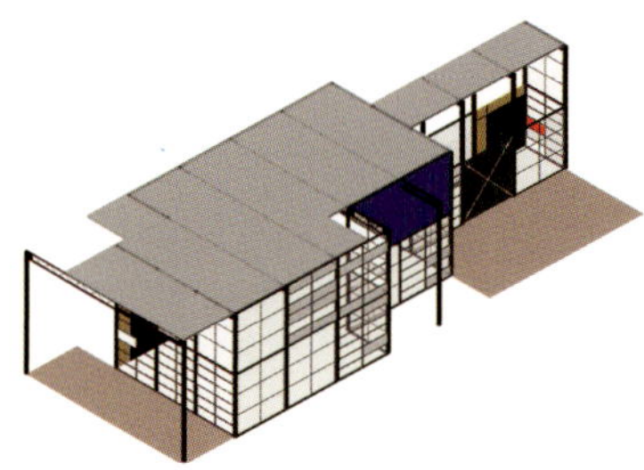

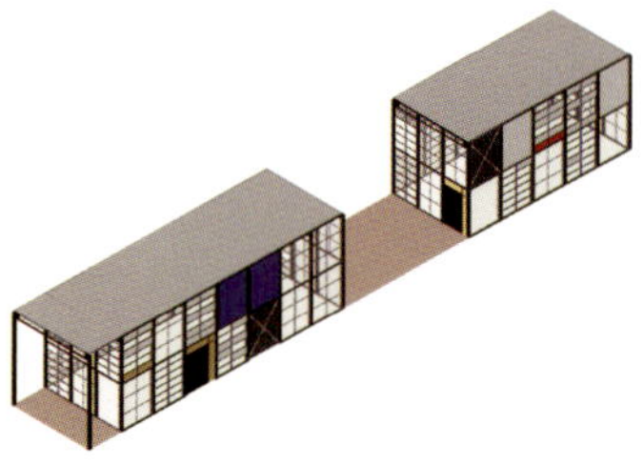

been a huge tendency towards collage-oriented manual two-dimensional post-processing of three-dimensional graphics. Take, for example, the entries from the "Digital/Mixed Category" of the Ken Roberts Memorial Architectural Delineation Competition. In the 2005-06 edition, (Fig. 4) everything is very glossy, graphic, and precise. But by the 2011-12 competition, (Figs. 5-7) there's an increasing inflection of dirt, construction lines, and atmosphere – a kind of 'personal touch'. This stimulates creativity and allows you to edit beyond merely applying a filter on top of the drawing that's already in the computer.

The next question – and this is the most crucial one – is the question of ambiguity.

In his *New York Times* article, Michael Graves talks about a game he used to play during boring Princeton faculty meetings, where he would be passing a drawing back and forth to his colleagues. He then hands it to Tony Vidler, who draws a stair at exactly the wrong scale – 20 times too big. It may seem like a joke, but these ambiguities can actually be productive. In my academic experience, half the time the critics would love a drawing because they ***misunderstood*** it – they saw something in it that its author had not intended.

There's something really powerful about ambiguity, and we don't often tap into it, because digital platforms don't do ambiguity that well. This gets back to the question of post-processing. In my own pieces, I sometimes take the direct 3-dimensional output of a generative script, then edit it as a 2-dimensional graphic to suppress certain aspects and bring out others. This ties into the "moving exchange" that Lewis Tsurumaki Lewis talk about: it's not just about post-processing; it's about allowing modifications you make to a two-dimensional graphic to return in, and inform, a three-dimensional problem.

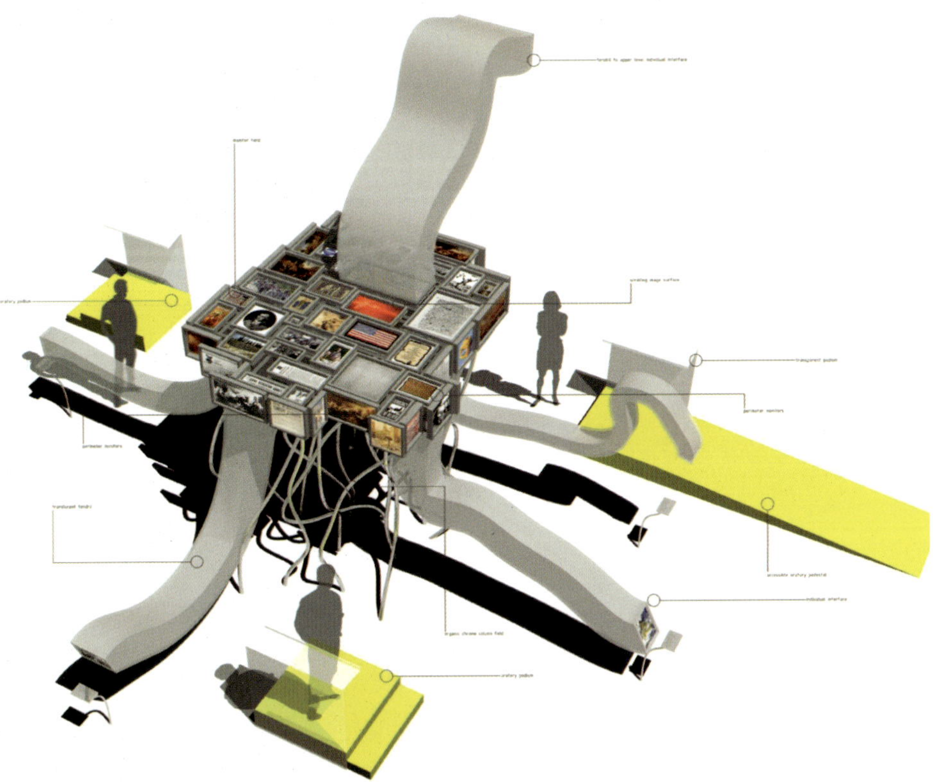

4 AIA Dallas Ken Roberts Memorial Delineation Competition, 2006: Finalist entry by Gail Peter Borden AIA. https://krobarch.com/winners#2006

5-7 AIA Dallas Ken Roberts Memorial Delineation competition, 2011-12: selected premiated entries by Robert Gilson, Tyler Bornstein and Miles Gertler. https://www.krobarch.com/winners.php#2011

8 Andrew Heumann, Preparatory Rendering for *Abstraction II*, 2011

9 Andrew Heumann, *Abstraction II*, Digital Image, 2011

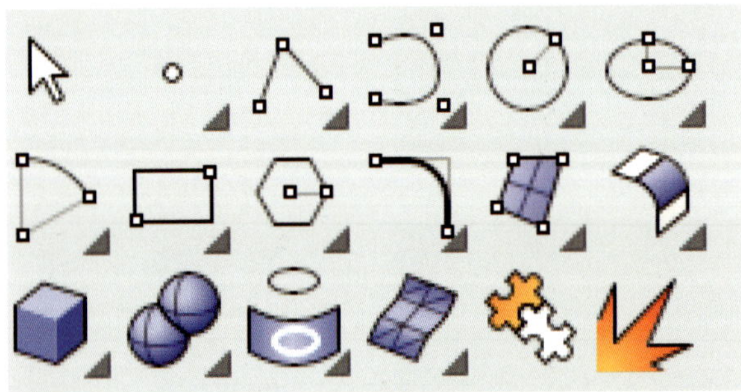

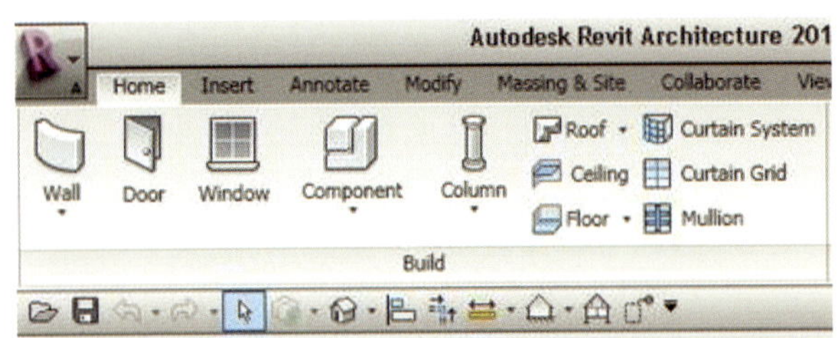

10-11 Above: Tool menu, McNeel Rhino 5.0 visualization software. Below: Tool menu, Autodesk Revit.

Geometry:
 Valid point.
 Point at (7.03473,14.0373,5.27296).
 Geometry UserData:
  UserData ID: 3B7FB506-437C-431e-B1D7-93C4CBFF417F

12 Embedded Data, screenshot from McNeel Rhino 5.0

A major problem with digital platforms such as Rhino, Revit and AutoCAD is that they set up ontologies: *What are 'objects'? What are the things you can draw?* Platforms that *limit* the entities you can work with are more productive of ambiguity. In something like Photoshop, where really the pixel is the basic entity, it's possible to make blurry representations. But it's very hard in Revit to make something that's *partially a door* and *partially a window* or, in Rhino, something that's *kind of a curve* and *kind of a surface*.

Another aspect of this is *dimensional precision*. If you draw a point in Rhino of some absurdly precise 3-dimensional location, this information remains accessible as you're working in a 3D platform. In order for digital platforms to open up the possibility of ambiguity, it's important to actually *suppress* the underlying data representation, in order to hold back information. When you're drawing a sketch, there *is* no automatic dimension. You can take out a ruler, but it's not embedded in the information that's being produced.

The situation today is frequently characterised as a contrast between the analogue – two-dimensional, physical, intuitive that involves manual processes – and the digital, which is three-dimensional, automatic, generative, precise and virtual. But the inherent qualities of drawing that make it such a valuable tool for creative production are not limited to analog media. They can be imported into digital media. There may even be ways to inflect digital intelligence, via augmented reality or other platforms, back onto a typical process of sketching.

Practices of design tend to concentrate at either end of these two poles, but there's a huge fertile ground in the middle in which full-on hybrids could be produced where something could be digital but intuitive and two-dimensional, or three-dimensional but analog and automatic. I think many of these practices already exist, but there's still a tendency to view things in a polarized way.

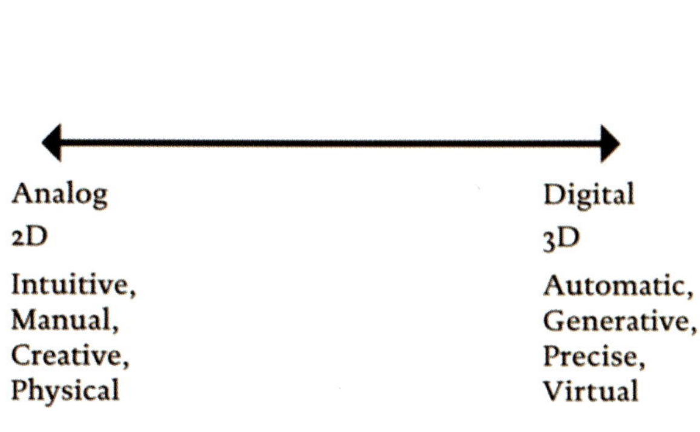

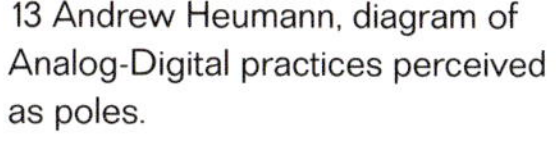
13 Andrew Heumann, diagram of Analog-Digital practices perceived as poles.

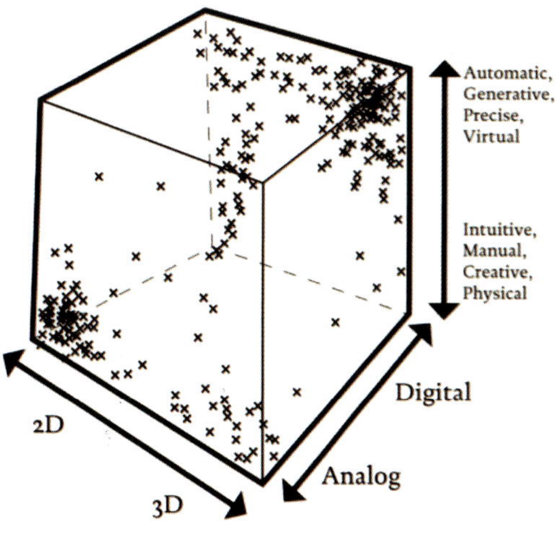

14 Andrew Heumann, diagram of potential Analog-Digital hybrids.

On Drawing

Seher Shah

1 Seher Shah, *Untitled (Wall)*, 2010.
Graphite and gouache on paper,
183 cm x 183 cm.

When I think of drawing, I think of both art and architecture, and how these two fields have given me a space to practice my work. Growing up in London, Brussels, Lahore and New York allowed me to experience different types of architectural spaces at a young age. This interest led to an education in the fine arts as well as a degree in architecture. My education was furthered by working in an architecture office that specialized in large-scale urban projects and skyscrapers as objects in the city. My practice uses this experience from art and architecture to think about space, landscape, objects and aesthetics through drawing, printmaking and sculpture. In recent years I find myself thinking about the language of drawing and how to represent an experiential nature of space. The relationships within perspective drawings, the aesthetics of architecture, and materiality within drawing and sculpture are some of the preoccupations in my practice.

Perspective drawing

My education as an architect taught me the tools of architectural representation, such as plan, section, elevation and perspective, and how to think about space and form three-dimensionally. This led to a series of large-scale perspective drawings that explored a number of ideas; attitudes towards place, time and geography; the nature of public and private space; utopian city plans; idealized modernist architecture and historical monuments and spectacles.

One of the aspects of perspective drawing, that is important to me, is the nature of public to private space. Oppositional relationships can break

2 Seher Shah, *Cross conference scheme* from the *Manual for Treason*, 2011. Digital print, 36 cm x 48 cm.

down within this drawing process. The public, or external, can reference historic events, iconic architecture and aesthetics. The private can be opaque, reticent and speaks about a different system, or attitude, towards the landscape. Drawing space can collapse this binary and becomes a way in which I can start to develop works.

In my drawings, I have used idealized modernist architecture, such as Le Corbusier's Unité d'habitation and the Capitol Complex in Chandigarh, as points of reference. My interest in these two geographically different projects was about the breaking down, isolating and manipulating of certain universal architectural components such as the wall, grid, window and threshold. *Object Relic (Unité d'habitation)* is a large-scale drawing that flattens the height and mass of the Unité building and situates the form in an ambiguously scaled landscape. The role of the architect, the use of scale and the contradictory principles inherent in this iconic work are a few of the reasons I was attracted to the project.

Aesthetics of architecture

Travel from an early age introduced me to a variety of aesthetics. From the Alhambra in Cordoba, the Grand Place in Brussels, the United Nations buildings in New York and to the Wazir Khan Mosque in Lahore, these early experiences of architecture and aesthetics left a strong impression. Reflecting different values, intentions, hierarchies and personal motivations, I became interested in these aesthetics, in ideas from modernism and their translation in different parts of the world. One of the aesthetics I have been researching in recent years is Brutalism.
There are contradictions inherent in this architectural aesthetic along with principles that involve landscape, social engineering and repetitive

3 Seher Shah, *Object Relic (Unité d'Habitation)*, 2011. Graphite and gouache on paper, 183 cm x 275 cm.

structural forms. Brutalist architecture with its initial utopian ideology has an ambiguous relationship to the landscape. It is an aesthetic that does not gently conform to the surrounding environment. It remains autonomous and independent. The drawing series ***Brutalist Traces*** uses horizontal graphite lines to render concrete sculptural forms in the landscape. Based on photographic images these drawings explore ideas of lightness, mass, erasure and weight through the material application of graphite. The buildings range from the Kuwait embassy in Tokyo, Barbican Estate in London to the Akbar Bhawan in New Delhi. Beyond aesthetics, I am interested in a more fundamental question about the use and limits of repetition: how far can repetition be imposed on society, community or people?

Material shifts from drawing to sculpture

Responding to the relationship between two to three dimensions has taken my drawings into sculpture. ***Hewn***, a series of woodcuts, uses the two-dimensional materiality of the ink on paper to develop forms using the removal of material. Taking these two-dimensional forms and extruding them into three-dimensions as small-scale objects developed into the ***Untitled*** cast iron works. Using the materiality of iron to think through ideas of surface materiality, the cut and weight were different thoughts coming into the work.

Drawing is a transformative process where I can use personal memory and attitudes alongside, or against, the status quo of the iconic and historic. I construct perspectives not just as a drawing method, but as a process that allows for disaffected elements alongside the idealism inherent within architectural aesthetics.

4 Seher Shah, *Capitol Complex (split line courtyard)*, 2012. Collage on paper, 28 cm x 36 cm.

5 Seher Shah, *Brutalist Traces (Akbar Bhawan I – New Delhi)*, 2015. Graphite on paper, 127 cm x 102 cm.

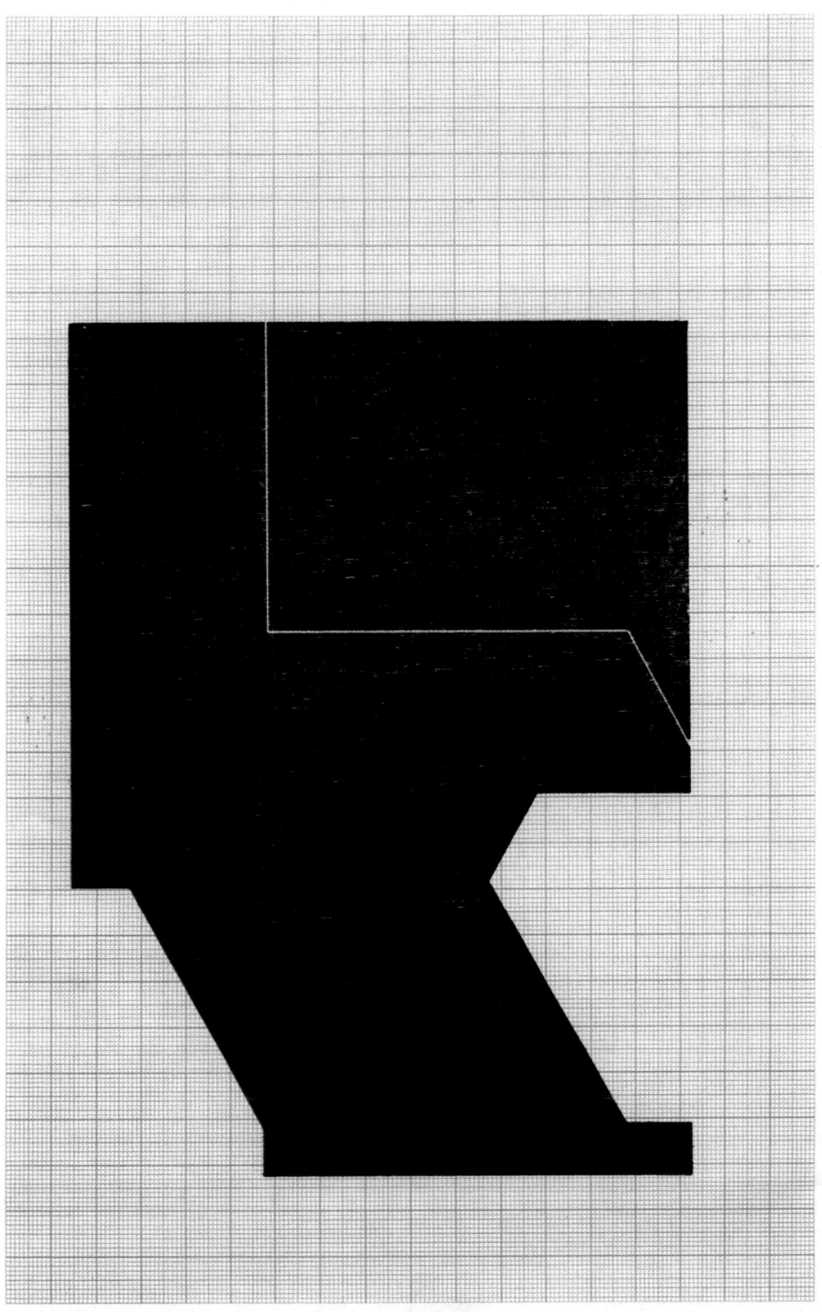

6 Seher Shah, *Hewn (cantilever cut), 2014*. Woodcut on A4 grid paper. 30 cm x 21 cm. Monoprint.

Between Accident and Control: Contrasting Traditions of Computational Design

Daniel Cardoso Llach

1 A reconstruction of Ivan Sutherland's 1964 "Sketchpad" system, the first interactive graphics system, sits alongside *Blooms Day*, a 1969 generative painting by George Stiny, in *Designing the Computational Image, Imagining Computational Design*, an exhibition curated by Daniel Cardoso Llach in 2017 at the Miller Gallery, Pittsburgh.

Not 'just another tool'

Since architects began to flirt with computers in the 1960s, debates about the role of computation in architecture have often been framed antagonistically – as arenas for technophobes and technophiles to clash, each staking a claim on the unique value, or promise, of their respective practices. This dichotomy is tempting. On the one hand, images of automated design systems – offering creative freedom, managerial efficiency, or 'personalized' design solutions – abound in architecture's six-decades romance with computation. Seductive and often reductive, these images outlined the contours of a computationally augmented practice of architecture, and captured the imagination of many architects in academia and industry, effectively ushering an entire academic sub-field.

Computers were greeted more cautiously, on the other hand, by those architects who saw them either as means of producing ineffective simulacra, or as a dangerously transformative force in architecture. For some in this group, computer screens simply failed to approximate the plasticity of sketches drawn by hand, or the tactility of a physical model; for others – aware of the social and organizational tensions introduced by technologies – computers conjured (not entirely unjustified) pre-industrial fears of automation, de-skilling and alienation.

A sort of bargain was thus struck across these seemingly distant intellectual territories: the idea that the computer is 'just another tool' that architects can utilize in their design process – another paintbrush or easel in the architect's atelier. Frequently deployed in studio reviews, 'think pieces' and course syllabi, this concept has become part of many architects' conventional wisdom, configuring a comfortable middle ground where computational ideas and techniques can co-exist with (albeit at a safe distance from) architecture's *hard core*.

My argument here is that, rather than clarifying, the 'just another tool' discourse obfuscates the truly important questions concerning computation in architecture. By casting hand-drawings and computer-generated images as *symmetrical*, it renders the very specificity of computation – a domain of analysis with historical and cultural depth – invisible. If we are to understand and address the contemporary entanglement of computation with architecture's long standing intellectual traditions and embodied practices, we must make computation *visible* and challenge the dichotomy that forces us to see it as either a threat to architecture's core, or as the protagonist of all-encompassing historical turn.

One of the numerous consequences of the 'just another tool' blind spot is the encouragement of unproductively nostalgic 'post-digital' attitudes. More importantly, by framing computers as 'just another tool' we make the *infrastructural scale* of computational design technologies invisible, and thus postpone, rather than address, a crucial debate.[1]

In this essay I want to focus on specificity, difference, and (to borrow a term from aeronautics) the *dissymmetries* between hand and computer drawing. The crucial difference between computer-generated images and hand drawings is that the former have *structure*.

1 Cardoso Llach, Daniel, *Builders of the Vision: Software and the Imagination of Design*. London: Routledge, 2015.

We may visualize this through an architectural metaphor. In a building, the structure is the rigid skeleton – usually made of wood, steel, or concrete – that makes it stand. Similarly, a computer drawing is unthinkable without an underlying structure. This structure is made not of wood or steel but of *symbols*; it is computable and numerical, and is encoded in the non-pictorial languages used by computers and software: it is made of code.

Similar to a building whose structure is concealed beneath cladding and paint, the structure of a computer drawing is hidden from view, and is fundamentally different from image itself. This becomes obvious when we consider how different the symbols are from the image we see glowing on the screen.

This decoupling of the image and its structure is not an opinion, nor a theoretical construction, nor a value judgment. It is the fundamental fact of computer graphics – and the crucial, irreducible difference between hand and computer 'drawings'. Compared to computer-generated images, hand drawings have no structure. As CAD pioneer Ivan Sutherland notably put it, "they are only dirty marks on paper."[2] Acknowledging this distinction helps dispel the deceptive symmetry of the 'just another tool' discourse, and allows us to examine the issues at stake in more detail, and makes the instruments involved in computational design ***visible.*** I am speaking, of course, of software and, more specifically, of the software interfaces that strongly condition architectural labors today by structuring the experience of computation for users. Software interfaces shape the way computation's own materialities – electrons, switches, logic gates, machine code, data structures, and software functions, roughly in that order of abstraction – intertwine with the materialities of design and thus are important to our analysis (Fig 2).

Rather than as pawns in a tired culture-war, we ought to see software and software interfaces as active participants in the worlds of architecture – in fact, as the very infrastructure of many architectural activities – and as historically and culturally situated theories of design.[3] In an attempt to shift the focus of the discussion, in this short essay I will sketch some underpinnings of software ***qua*** theory of design in architecture by discussing two distinct intellectual traditions of computational design.

2 Sutherland, Ivan, "Structure in Drawing and the Hidden-Surface Problem," in *Reflections on Computer Aids to Design and Architecture*, edited by Nicholas Negroponte, 73-77 (excerpt not including the "hidden surface problem"). New York, 1975. I discuss the question of structure in the computational image in Cardoso Llach, Daniel, "Architecture and the Structured Image: Software Simulations as Infrastructures for Building Production" in *Operative Artifacts: Imagery in the Age of Modeling*, Sabine Ammon, Inge Hindterwaldner, eds. Springer, 2017.

3 For a discussion of the notion of software as theory of design, see Cardoso Llach, Daniel, "Software Comes to Matter: Towards a Material History of Computational Design," *DesignIssues* 31, no. 3, Summer 2015: 41–55. https://doi.org/10.1162/DESI_a_00337.

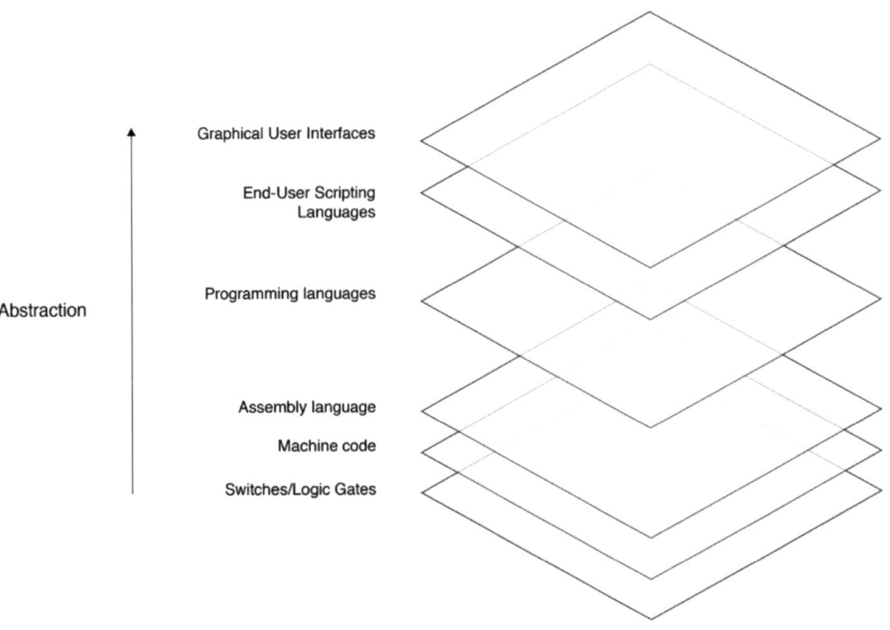

2 Diagram representing the varying levels of abstraction of computational systems. The higher levels of abstraction, such as Graphical User Interfaces, are typically both human-readable and hardware-agnostic.
Image: Daniel Cardoso Llach.

The Algorithmic Aesthetics Tradition

The first I shall call the 'Algorithmic Aesthetics' tradition.[4] Influenced by Noam Chomsky's theory of Generative Grammars in linguistics, and by George Birkhoff's numerical theory of aesthetics, German Philosopher Max Bense first formulated the concept of "generative aesthetics" in an influential 1965 manifesto.[5] Bense, who was based in the University of Stuttgart, Germany, saw computers as vehicles of aesthetic investigation. His teachings helped spur a generation of pioneers – including Frieder Nake, Georg Nees and Vera Molnar – who used early pen-plotters to produce some of the earliest examples of computer-generated art. Often using pseudo-random numbers to determine the placement of visual elements in their compositions, the work of these early computer artists hinges on a delicate balance between regularity and disorder (Fig 3).

Their work was received with skepticism by the art world. Two factors may help explain this resistance. On the one hand, its procedural nature challenged conventional understandings of artistry, skill, and authorship. On the other, an influential segment of the artistic establishment of Post-War Europe saw these artworks as byproducts of the war machine: outputs of chiefly militaristic – and often US – technologies, or seductive honey traps set-up by ruthless forces of production. Despite the skepticism it encountered initially (some of which persists today), the work of these artists was echoed by other artists and architects; it had a considerable impact on design culture and education (for example through figures like architect and computer graphics pioneer John Lansdown in the UK) and is widely recognized as pioneering today.

In the United States, the Algorithmic Aesthetics tradition in visual design can be traced the most clearly to the work by George Stiny and James Gips, whose

4 "Algorithmic Aesthetics" is the title of a 1978 book by George Stiny and James Gips. "Algorithmic Aesthetics: Computer Models for Criticism and Design in the Arts," *Algorithmic Aesthetics*, 1978, http://www.algorithmicaesthetics.org/. I borrow this title here to refer to works that include Stiny and Gips' work as well as the work of others.

5 See Bense, Max. "The project of generative aesthetics", 1965.

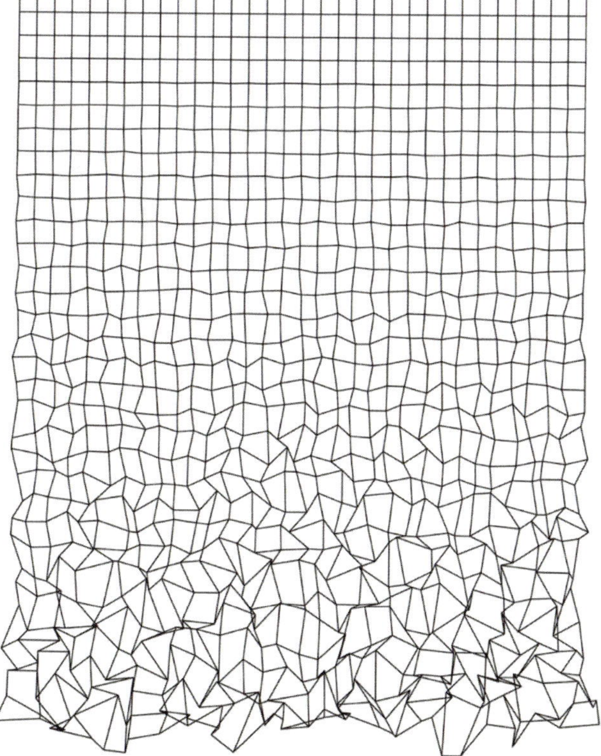

3 In a course taught by the author at Penn State University, students reconstructed early works of software art. This image is a 2013 reconstruction in the Processing language of *Aesthetic Unrest: Dispersion of Squares* (1968) by computer art pioneer Georg Nees. Reconstruction by Seoug Oh.

seminal 1971 paper on Shape Grammars spoke of the "generative specification of painting and sculpture."[6] Like Bense's information aesthetics, Stiny's and Gips mathematical definition of design as a rule-based visual and perceptual calculation invoked Chomsky's and Birkhoff's ideas, and resonated with other contemporary intersections of mathematics and art.[7] Because of their capacity to act as descriptive, analytic, and generative visual systems, Shape Grammars triggered a school of design practice and scholarly thought that continues to evolve today.

Among the myriad cultures of computational design that have developed over the last several decades, many evoke the Algorithmic Aesthetics tradition. These cultures have often evolved in conjunction with open source software development languages such as Processing and Open Frameworks,[8] and are as diverse intellectually as they are technologically. Their members' complicated disciplinary identities are often amalgams of graphic, interaction, and architectural design, as well as advertising and new media art. The lively "New Aesthetic" conversation, which debated the cultural significance of computing in the arts the late 2000s and early 2010s, reflects this sensibility. Architectural expressions of the Algorithmic Aesthetics tradition may seem hard to find at first, but they abound, especially among architectural theorists and researchers. Aside from the significant body of descriptive and analytical work in architectural studies related to Shape Grammars, researchers since the 1960s have used computation to explore 'design spaces' defined through combinatorics and enumeration; to produce non-deterministic formal or material effects; and to elicit unconventional configurational logics. **(Figs. 4 and 5)** Cambridge architect and researcher Phillip Steadman offers a crisp illustration of this sensibility when he defines architecture as "the science of possible forms."[9]

The detailed explication of these subfields could be the subject of an entire dissertation. What is key for this analysis is that for artists, architects, designers and researchers working within the Algorithmic Aesthetics tradition, computation

6 George Stiny and James Gips, "Shape Grammars and the Generative Specification of Painting and Sculpture" in *Segmentation of Buildings for 3D Generalisation. Proceedings of the Workshop on Generalisation and Multiple Representation*, Leicester, 1971.

7 For a discussion on the new forms of authorial agency emerging as a result of machine learning and data, see Cardoso Llach, Daniel, "Data as Interface: The Poetics of Machine Learning in Design," in *Machine Learning. Medien, Infrastrukturen Und Technologien Der Künstlichen Intelligenz (Machine Learning. Media, Infrastructures and Technologies of Artificial Intelligence)*. Transcript, 2018.

8 To a significant extent, these cultures are traceable to the 1990s work of the Aesthetics and Computation Group at the MIT MediaLab. Among these, the community of creative coders around Processing is particularly strong. Processing is a computer language derived from Java designed to simplify complex aspects of programming in order to making it accessible to visual artists and designers across fields. See, for example, Casey Reas and Ben Fry, *Processing: A Programming Handbook for Visual Designers and Artists*, Second Edition, Cambridge, Massachusetts: MIT Press, 2015.

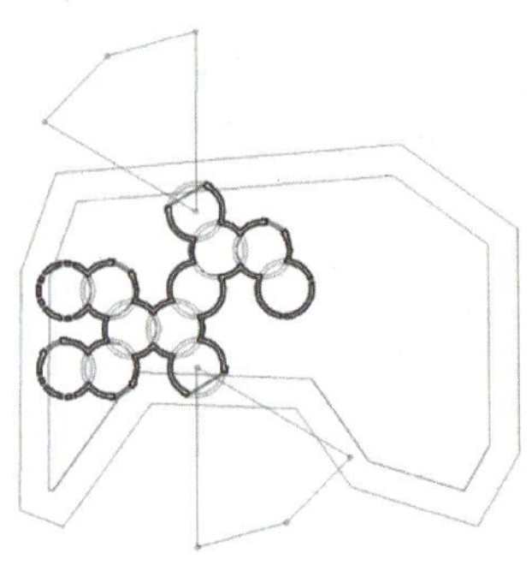

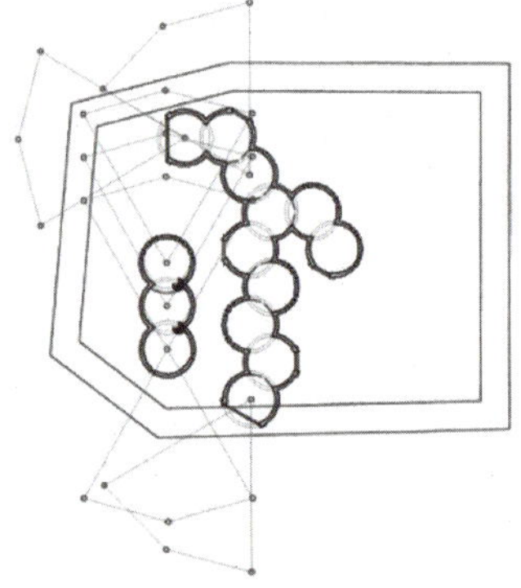

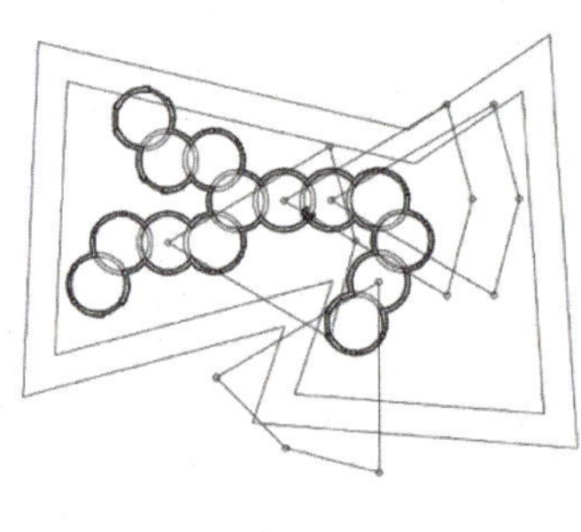

4 The Melnikov Grammar is an experimental computer program that implements a shape grammar to generate architectural plans following stylistic traits of Russian architect Konstantin Melnikov procedurally and non-deterministically.
Image and software credit: Daniel Cardoso Llach.

appears as a new, open-ended medium with its own expressive, material and technical capacities and constraints. These constraints manifest through specific computational approaches to design including formal systems, stochastic methods, and statistical methods. In their work, computation does not appear as a surrogate for drawing or other forms of design, but as a new actor with entirely different dramatic potential.

9 Transactions of the Martin Centre for Architectural and Urban Studies, University of Cambridge, Volume 4, 1980. Steadman, Phil and Janet Owers (ed.)

Architect and artist James Wines has described hand drawing as "the fertile territory of subliminal accident."[10] We may use those same words to describe those working within the Algorithmic Aesthetics tradition, for whom design is about using computation to orchestrate the conditions for the right accidents to happen.

10 See James Wines' essay, pp 38-49 in this volume.

The Algorithmic Tectonics Tradition

A second tradition of computational design engages differently – perhaps antagonistically – with the creative process. Instead of serendipity and accident, its proponents seek the safety of control. This tradition, which I shall call 'Algorithmic Tectonics,' is steeped in technique. The root ***tekton*** (carpenter in Greek) invokes its distinguishing trait: the understanding of computer-generated images as structured and engineered artifacts.[11] This sensibility was central to the development of the first interactive design systems. In contemporary architectural cultures, this tradition is discernible in the ambition to use computers to achieve increased managerial efficiency and control.

11 *Tekton* also registers archi***tecture***'s fundamental concern with material articulation.

The early development of Computer-Aided Design systems in the 1950s and 60s offers clues about the central motifs of the Algorithmic Tectonics tradition. As I discuss in detail elsewhere,[12] CAD systems originated in university laboratories from an engineering impulse to increase speed and efficiency in the design and manufacture of aircraft parts. An early ambition of CAD researchers was to develop symbolic languages capable of representing ***any*** design problem, and to re-imagine design itself in technological terms. Here, drawings were no longer drawn, but

12 For a detailed discussion of these questions, see Cardoso Llach, *Builders of the Vision*, op cit.

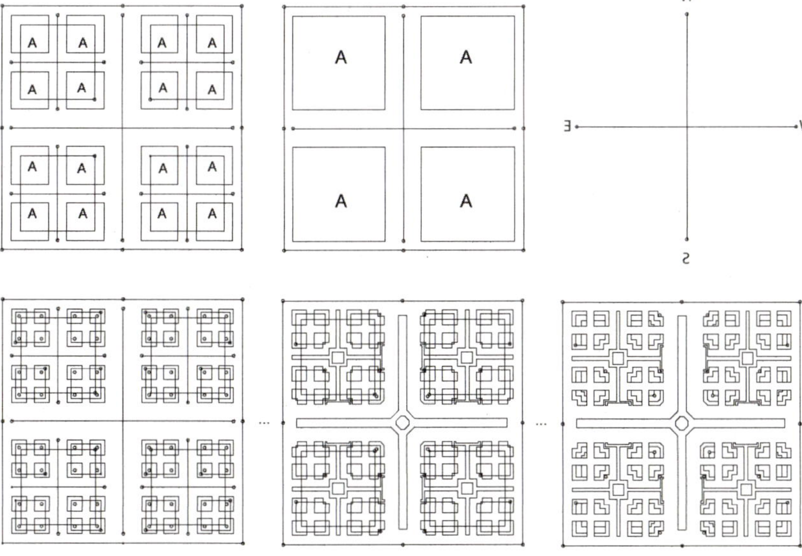

5 Mughal garden designs generated semi-automatically using GRAPE, a computer program for implementing parametric shape rules. Image Credit: Nirvik Saha. See Economou, Athanassios, and Thomas Grasl, "Paperless Grammars," in *Computational Studies on Cultural Variation and Heredity*, edited by Ji-Hyun Lee, 139–60. Singapore: Springer Singapore, 2018. https://doi.org/10.1007/978-981-10-8189-7_12.

built. Accordingly, the first CAD tools sought not merely to replicate traditional drawing methods, but rather to explore the specific capacities of the new platform. CAD pioneers such as Steven A. Coons and Douglas Ross, and their students, re-imagined the very concept of design in computational terms as an iterative process of representation, analysis, and materialization.[13]

13 Ibid.

The 'structure' of computer-generated images was central to their vision. Early CAD researchers understood that computational descriptions were less like drawings and more like databases. A geometric model of a house, for example, could be enriched with information about materials, prices, structural calculations, and other attributes. The data structures that encoded geometric information could be manipulated computationally, thus making drawings responsive to geometric and mathematical constraints. This new view of drawings as engineered artifacts allowed CAD theorists and advocates to claim that computer-generated images bore structural (not just pictorial) resemblance with the artifacts they described. It set in motion a technological imaginary of design and creativity that increasingly dominates present-day discussions about architectural production. (Fig. 6)

This engineering sensibility toward design representations, and its commitment to managerial control and efficiency, is the essence of the Algorithmic Tectonics tradition. Through multiple cultural and historical channels – not least CAD software itself – this ambition has permeated other design fields. Architects working on 'parametric design,' for example, take advantage of the structured nature of computer-generated models to stage design processes by modeling geometric and mathematical constraints. Architects working on 'Building Information Modeling' (BIM) organize their practice – along with other professions and trades – around an interactive computer simulation so as to reduce

6 Ivan Sutherland's Sketchpad is widely recognized as the first interactive graphics sofware, and as a template for CAD systems. The four drawings below were generated using a reconstruction of Sketchpad, developed by Daniel Cardoso Llach and Scott Donaldson in 2017.

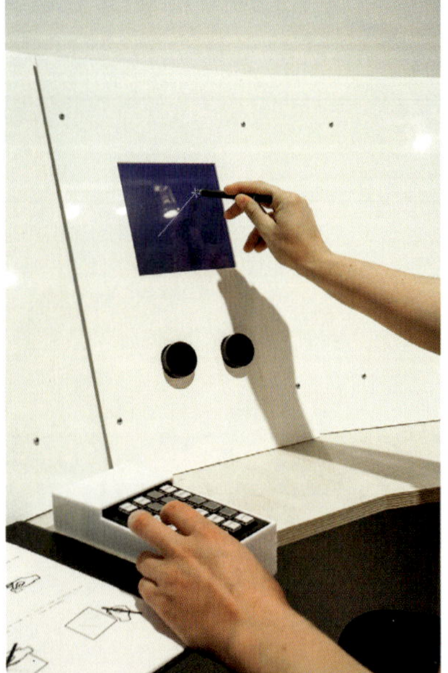

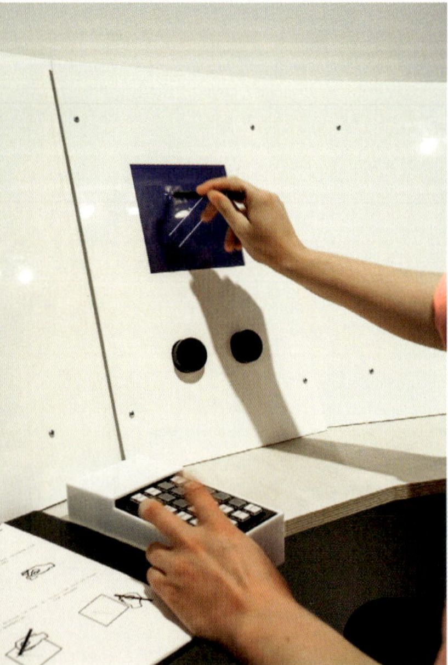

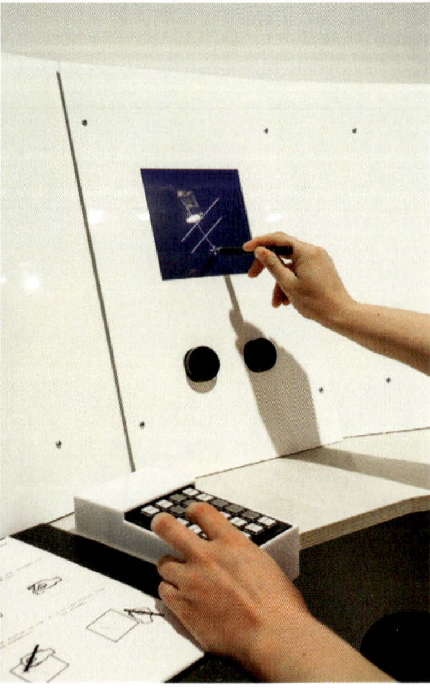

conflicts and improve communication.[14] (Fig 7) These forms of design production have gained a footing in architectural practice and education, sometimes with the aura of an inevitable 'wave'.

Conclusion

While in fact intertwined, the two intellectual traditions sketched in this short essay are expressions of distinct political histories, disciplinary identities, and aesthetic sensibilities. They manifest distinct (and divergent) ideas about design and representation. They outline specific ways in which computers are not 'just another tool' but rather vehicles of theoretical, aesthetic, and practical commitments in design. To call what designers do with computers 'drawing' risks confusing expectations and limiting possibilities.

We need a new vocabulary to do justice to the unruly landscapes of contemporary computational design practices. The two sketches in this essay attempt to enrich that vocabulary.

Where the Algorithmic Aesthetics tradition is concerned with accident, unpredictability, and authorial detachment, the Algorithmic Tectonics tradition is concerned with control, descriptive accuracy, and accountability. Where Algorithmic Aesthetics engages with open-endedness and serendipity, Algorithmic Tectonics optimizes and gives voice to our desire for certainty. Where Algorithmic Aesthetics thematizes *form,* Algorithmic Tectonics thematizes ***information.***

With this enriched vocabulary as a background, we may consider the pedagogical and practical demands of a forward-looking and computationally-literate approach to architecture in a new light.

14 Peter Galison has usefully observed that in the aftermath of the Second World War, computer simulations allowed scientists of different fields to collaborate, becoming a kind of "trading zone" for researchers without a shared disciplinary background. Galison, Peter, *Image and Logic: A Material Culture of Microphysics*, Chicago: University of Chicago Press, 1997.

15 For an extended discussion of this project see Cardoso Llach, Daniel, "Tracing Design Ecologies," in *Digital STS Handbook*, ed. Janet Vertesi and David Ribes, Princeton University Press, 2017, and Daniel Cardoso Llach, "Visualizing BIM Coordination," 2012, on vimeo.com: https://vimeo.com/51693897

7 These data visualizations represent different stages during the development of a large architectural project. Each line represents a design "conflict" reported during coordination. Software and image credit: Daniel Cardoso Llach, 2011.[15]

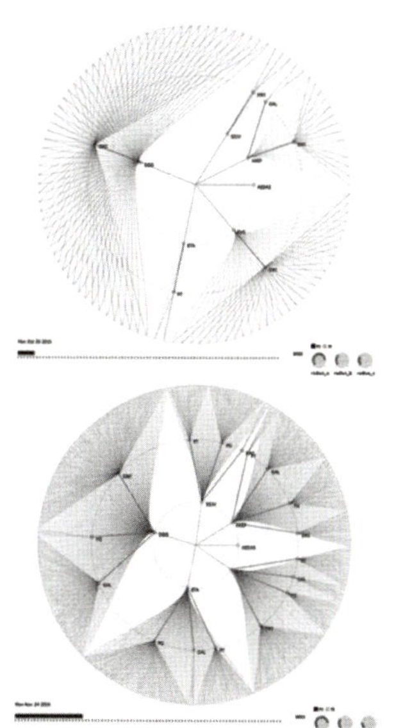

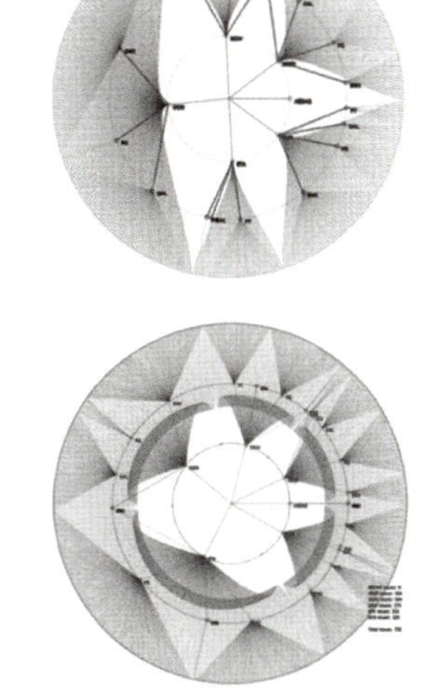

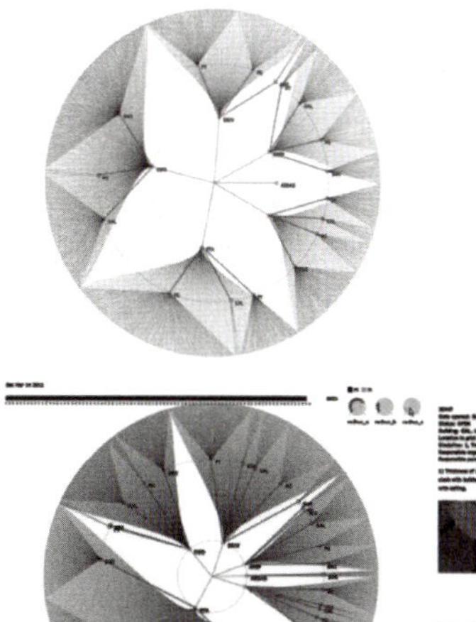

Jump Cuts

Ann Tarantino

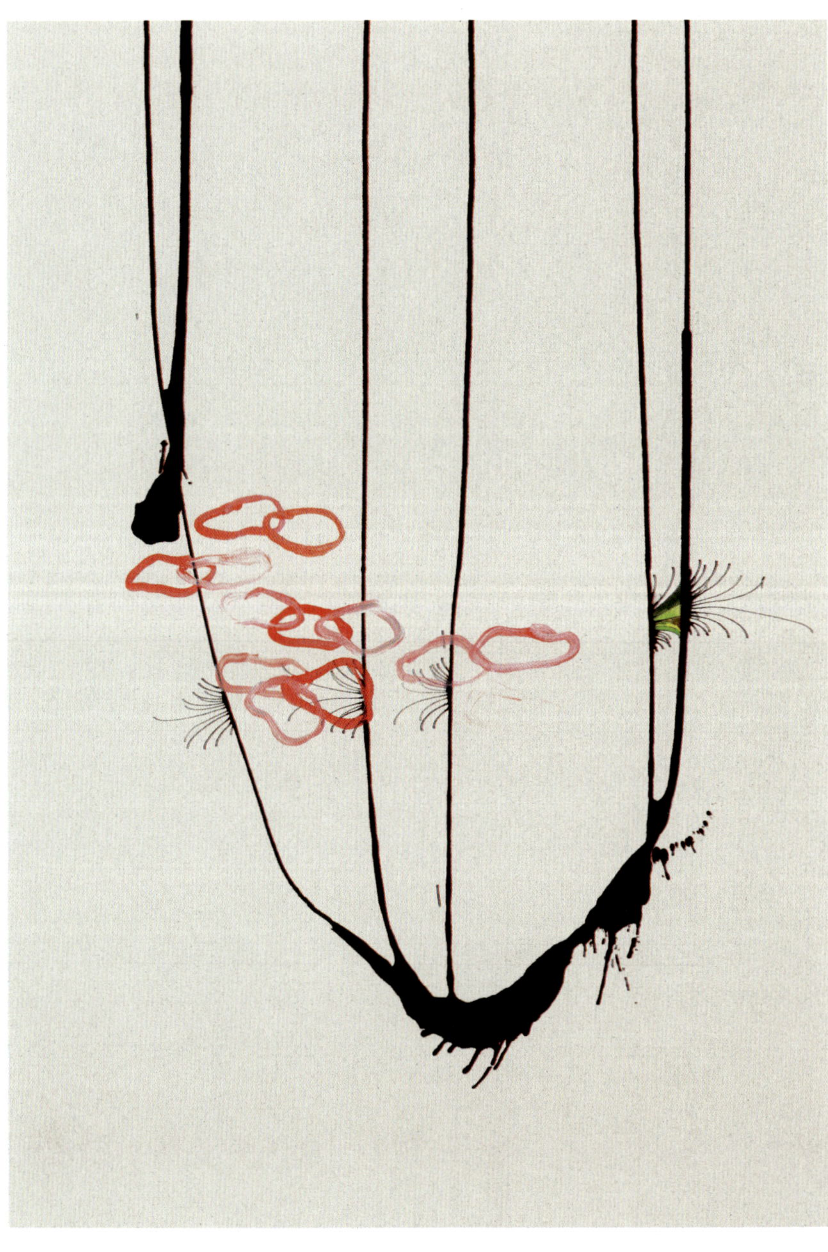

1 Ann Tarantino, *Breath Portrait (pink bubbles)*, 2007. Ink and gouache on paper, 61 cm x 76.2 cm.

When I first moved to New York after finishing my MFA, my very first job was working here at The Drawing Center – so today's symposium is a homecoming of sorts. Looking back, I realize that much of my understanding of what drawing can be – and much of my thinking about space – I gained from working on exhibitions here.

For example, the show *12 Views*, and in particular a piece by Claudia Schmacke, really impacted me. This was over 15 years ago, so it seemed more radical at the time, but I remember being struck by the way her piece had no interest whatsoever in being on the wall. She worked with plastic tubing filled with water, coiled in large circles on the gallery floor. Later, in the 2005 show *LineAge*, Monika Grzymala made tape installations that also dispensed with the wall altogether, responding to the physical and architectural space of the gallery. I fell in love with these works and also their particular way of describing, responding to, and impacting the space in which the viewer orbited around the work. Other shows included cyanotypes, cut paper and performances. Being surrounded by this work impacted my understanding of drawing and my desire to respond to space rather than depict it.

I left New York to live in Japan for a couple of years, where my thinking about space and how it could be constructed changed further. Looking at traditional woodblock prints, I became interested in how things could be simultaneously flat and spatial. Tourist maps of Kyoto, where I lived, weren't drawn to scale, but shifted according to the significance of the place or thing within the narrative. These scale shifts seemed to me to have a relationship to Chinese landscape painting, where the scale of objects is dependent upon relationships within a larger story rather than true scale. I found myself making works on paper influenced by these discoveries, with the kind of flatness and graphic quality in the print material I was surrounded by.

Ultimately this discovery led to my moving off of the page altogether– dispensing with paper and moving directly onto the walls of the gallery space. In 2009, I collaborated with fellow artist Kate McGraw on a site-specific piece in Washington DC. We drew on the ceiling, drew around the corners, on the floor, on the desk. It was an incredibly liberating opportunity.

2 Ann Tarantino (in collaboration with Kate McGraw), *Workbook*, 2009. Ink, charcoal, acrylic, and powdered pigment on walls and ceiling, dimensions variable.

Around this time, I started exploring different methods for moving ink across a large surface, which required something more than my hands. I settled on a low-tech tool: the air compressor, the kind you might use to clean out your garage. This led to a series of site-specific wall drawings, in which marks travel through and around each space, using the air compressor to move the ink. Working with the idiosyncrasies of quirky architectural spaces was exciting.

I've always been intrigued by visual languages other than those with which I'm already familiar. As an artist teaching in both the art and design schools at Penn State, I am continually influenced by the work of my students and my colleagues. This led me to the use of the laser cutter as another tool for mark-making. I took my old drawings and digitally traced them so that they became echoes of the previous images, and then etched those into paper, sometimes leaving little pinpricks in the paper so light could peek through. During the etching process, I manipulated each

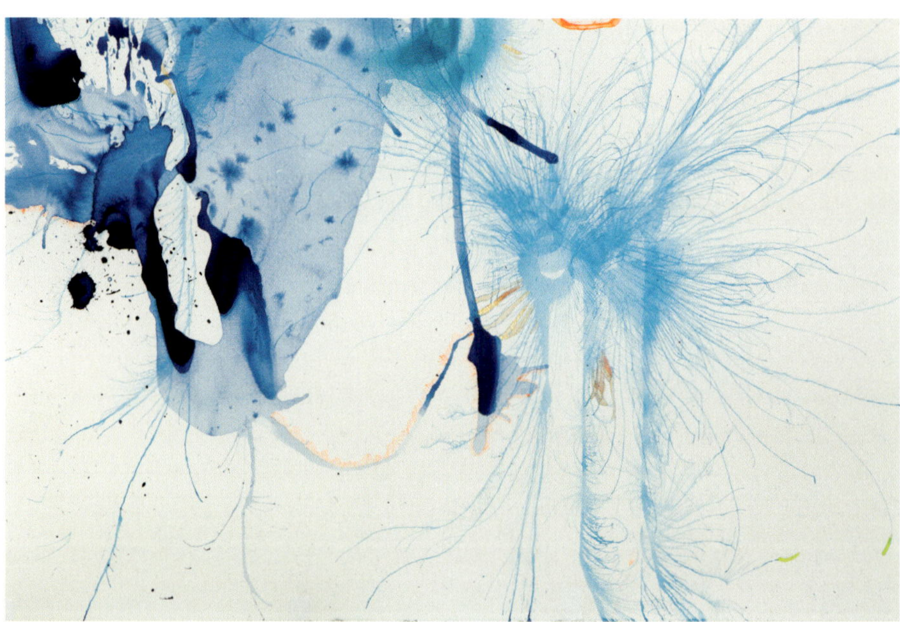

3 Ann Tarantino, *Big Blue* (detail), 2007. Ink and gouache on paper, 183 cm x 153 cm.

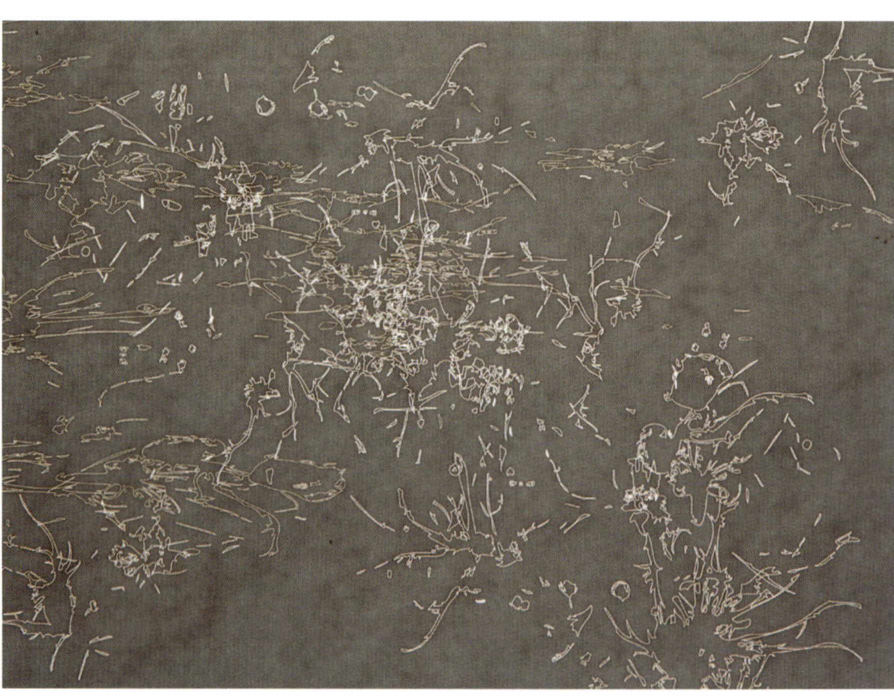

4. Ann Tarantino, *A Guide to Frost*, 2013. Laser-cut paper, 76 cm x 61 cm.

file further: stretching, elongating, stacking, layering and then finally cutting into the surface – eventually illuminating it from behind.

These works lie at an intersection of hand and machine because there's so much manipulation that goes into making them. It's not a matter of just generating an image, then executing and printing it. There's a lot of mediation that goes on, whether I'm turning the paper, flipping it, adjusting the speed of the laser cutter, adjusting the power, moving between engraving and actual cutting, and so forth.

Whether installed on light boxes or on windows, these pieces use light as a medium and are brought to life by ambient or direct light – whether sunlight or manufactured. The cast shadows start to carve out volumes of space on the floor. Looking back at these pieces, I see a simultaneous ***depth*** and ***removal of depth***. They're flat and also spatial at the same time – which brings me back again to Japanese prints, and the limitless options for how space can be drawn, defined and described.

5 Ann Tarantino, *Future Perfect*, 2013. Laser-cut paper and acetate on existing windows, 272 cm x 294 cm x 906 cm.

6 Ann Tarantino, *Topoanalysis*, 2013. Laser-cut paper on existing windows, 269 cm x 193 cm, 202 cm x 74 cm, and 202 cm x 136 cm.

Technology as Vocabulary / Discursive Machines

Jürg Lehni

My work in software, design, art and education is, at its core, about communicating an openness towards technology as a vocabulary and language that gives us the freedom to formulate processes and structures – rather than as a means for big corporations to fence us in as dutiful consumers.

During my studies in various fields ranging from electronic engineering to interaction design and media art[1], I started working collaboratively with other designers on a series of screen-based projects that questioned the role of off-the-shelf software in the creative process[2]. Each project took a graphical element or principle and made its visual exploration intuitive and playful, thereby emphasizing the often-unperceived limitations of predominant commercial software. When some of these experiments were selected by Swiss graphic designer Cornel Windlin to be displayed as interactive type specimens on Lineto.com, he challenged us to move them away from the realm of software parody and turn them into useful tools, by adding the capacity to export real printable vector graphics.

Seemingly impossible at first, we gradually achieved this by reverse-engineering the format of Adobe Illustrator vector graphics files – a foray that led me to discover the mathematical and geometric beauty of Bézier curves, and would ultimately take me beyond the computer screen altogether. I became fascinated with the idea of opening up Adobe Illustrator to access all its curve-processing powers, so as to offer a meta-tool that would allow its users to create their own bespoke tools.

I was studying interaction design at ECAL at the time, but with a strong focus on graphic design, facilitated by the proximity to the university's very Swiss graphic design department, with which it shared a curriculum. There was a celebration of the computer aesthetic –people were fascinated by vector graphics and explored them playfully in their work – but with limited awareness of the impact of the software tools themselves on their work. (Andrew Heumann also spoke about this lack of depth.) As a designer – which is what I intended to become – I wanted control over the medium or the production facility, to render their role and influences visible.

In response to this realization, I launched Scriptographer in 2001. Installed as a software plug-in inside Adobe Illustrator, like a parasite or symbiont inside its corporate host, this program allowed users to create their own bespoke design tools using JavaScript, a simple scripting language designers had started to become familiar with through exposure to web technologies. Maintaining Scriptographer, teaching with it, and building/supporting a community of users through its website would keep me busy over the next 11 years. In 2008, the program became the topic of an ECAL research project in collaboration with Jonathan Puckey, one of its most avid users and contributors.[3]

1 I studied Electronic Engineering at ETH, Zürich from 1998-99, then studied Interaction Design and Media Art at HyperWerk, Basel (1999-2001) and ECAL, Lausanne (1999-2004).

2 Casio Font Watch (1999), Lego Font Creator (2000) and *Vectorama.org* (2000) were created in collaboration with my brother Urs Lehni and Rafi Koch, both then studying and later working as graphic designers in Lucerne. Rubik Maker (2000) was created in collaboration with Cornel Windlin for Lineto.com.

3. Jürg Lehni, "Teaching in the Spaces between Code and Design," *Eye* No 81, Autumn 2011. http://www.eyemagazine.com/feature/article/teaching-in-the-spaces-between-code-and-design). Jonathan Puckey and I have since continued working on *Paper.js*, a software framework that shares many of Scriptographer's key philosophies, without the risk of such corporate dependency.

For my ECAL graduation project in 2002, I decided to engage vector graphics through more than software: Bézier curves (their core components) are mathematical functions of time: they describe the trajectory of a point that, in its displacement over time, turns into a line or a curve. Or as Paul Klee said: "A line is a dot that went for a walk." What if this information could be leveraged to control the gestures not only of bespoke software but also of bespoke mark-making hardware–devices that came to life by conveying mathematically abstract, yet very concrete information?

At the time, Bézier curves were mostly used to place pixels on a screen, or instruct a printer to place dots of ink or toner on paper. Many older pen-based plotters, like those found in architecture and drafting firms, essentially followed sequences of lines as they were executed on paper.

I was after a more poetic expression: a device that could hold a tool the way a person would, carefully moving it over the surface as it follows mathematical instructions, but in a constant struggle with the mechanical reality of the task, with gravity, inertia and friction – a friction also between the perfect abstract information and its flawed execution as it becomes manifested in space. Without fully realizing at the time, I was becoming interested in building devices with unique character and gestural expression, a kind of personal media.

Two months before my ECAL diploma project was due, I started a dialogue with my friend Uli Franke, an engineer whom I had met at ETH. During this

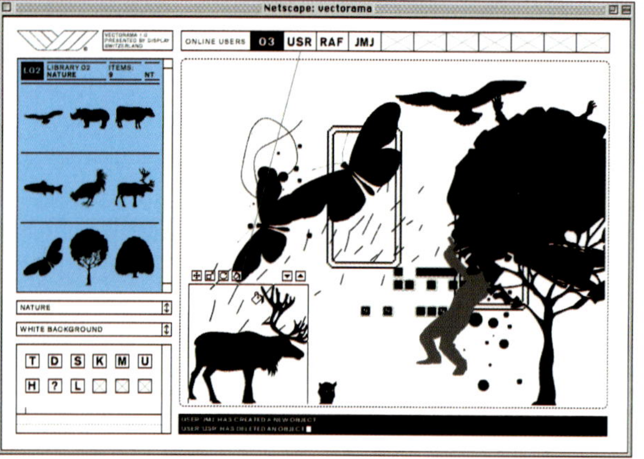

1 Jürg Lehni, Vectorama.

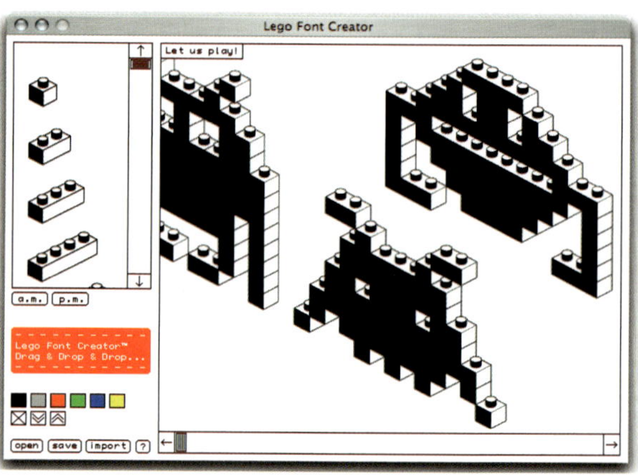

2 Jürg Lehni, Lego Font Creator, 2000.

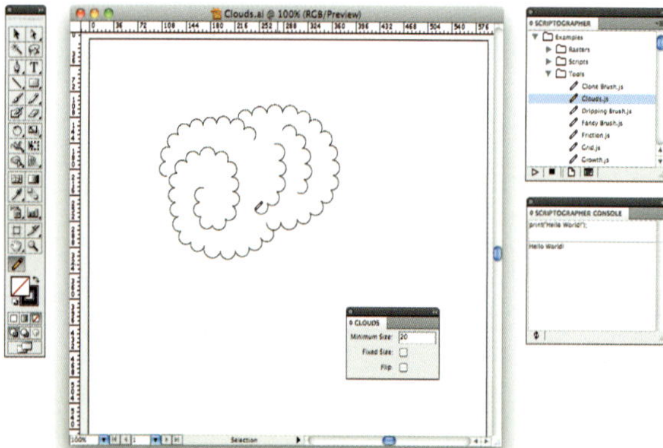
3 Jürg Lehni, Scriptographer, 2001-2012. Open-source scripting plug-in for Adobe Illustrator, available for free at http://scriptographer.org.

Ping Pong of ideas on the concept of imprecise media, the Eureka moment came when we moved an element from one unrealized plan up onto an imaginary wall. Suddenly, rather than being precisely controlled by mechanics, we could envisage a tool suspended from cables, positioned by a delicate and fragile triangulation of the forces involved. Hektor, the spray paint output device, was born. Now we simply had to build its mechanical and electronic body, and give it behavior through software.

In summer 2002 – long before the existence of affordable 3D printing or laser cutting – we hand-sawed parts out of plexiglas in Uli's kitchen. He etched and soldered the circuit board, while I adapted Scriptographer so it could speak to hardware. I developed algorithms to control and move the spray paint can, which would hang from toothed belts, positioned by wall-mounted stepper motors receiving digital instructions. For the first time, my work in software would escape the screen, and there was something very exciting about it. But there were also some surprises in store.

Our original plan was to position the spray paint can with a motor in each corner of the drawing surface, with four belts forming an 'X' holding the spray-paint can at their intersection. But technical limitations in our design forced us to abandon the lower two motors and trust our instincts that gravity alone could be used to position the tool with sufficient precision. Not only did it work, it became one of a few lucky accidents which – combined with modifications to the software

4 Jürg Lehni and Dexter Sinister, *Hektor meets Dexter Sinister*, Swiss Institute, New York, 2007.

5 Jürg Lehni, Hektor, installation view in *Design and the Elastic Mind*, *Museum of Modern Art, New York, February 24-May 12, 2008.*

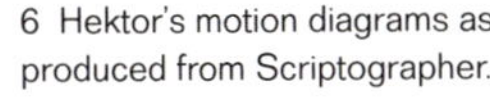

6 Hektor's motion diagrams as produced from Scriptographer.

8 Jürg Lehni and Ulli Franke at work producing *We Try Harder* for Cornel Windlin's contribution to the exhibition *Public Affairs* at Kunsthaus Zürich, 2002.

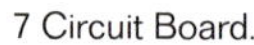

7 Circuit Board.

9 Spray Test.

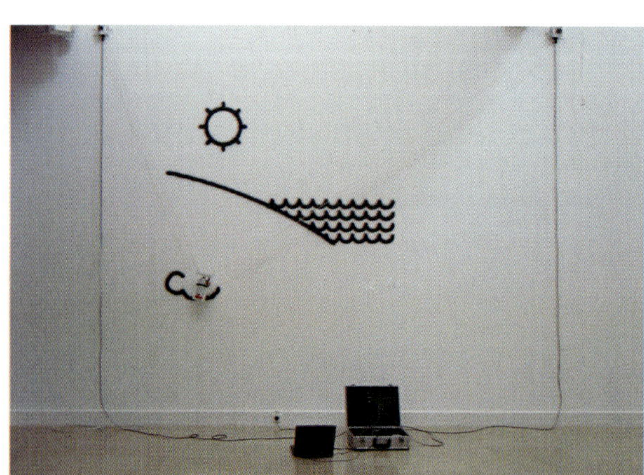

10 Jürg Lehni and Alex Rich, *Hektor Draws a Landscape, Lee 3 Tau Ceti Central Armory Show,* Villa Arson, Nice, 2003.

11 William Holder and Jürg Lehni, *Hektor Meets William Morris,* in *Tourette's II,* Gallery W139, Amsterdam, 2003

to prevent excess trembling – ultimately gave the machine its unique gestural quality.

Our solutions were not the most efficient in engineering terms, but this was not intended as an engineering project. Our mental model was to treat Hektor like a car without brakes, trying to draw on the ground while driving at a steady pace, and staying on smooth trajectories without any sudden turns. The resulting device had the character of a slightly nervous and hesitant painter planning their next strokes, the brush hovering above the canvas.

Hektor was intended as a device for producing wall-drawings with a very specific aesthetic. But after putting the machine to work, its true potential became apparent. As the authors of its hardware and software components, we had not anticipated that the contraption in motion would have a personality.

At a time when instructions are increasingly shared digitally and replicated across the globe, and the Maker Movement in the ascendant, the concepts of authorship and attribution become increasingly blurred in successive iterations of a project, as people start making their own versions. But our collaborative process of invention and discovery made it difficult for us to share this personal project as a concept available for reproduction by others. Questions of authorship were crucial to our experience of creating Hektor, and became central to what followed.

From its first public display at Kunsthaus Zürich in 2002,[4] Hektor captivated viewers' attention. At once spectacle and instrument, it opened unexpected doors, and sent us on a journey through the design and art worlds. We started to collaborate with several other designers and artists in a quest to find a voice for this machine, and things it could say. Hektor revealed the idea of the choreographed drawing: the instrumentalization of the sequence by which a drawing is created over time by a storytelling machine. I added new tools to my growing repertoire of Scriptographer scripts, to create narratives in drawing sequences that would be mesmerizing to watch as they unfolded. I also began to envision machines with other capabilities.

4. Cornel Windlin with Jürg Lehni and Uli Franke, *We Try Harder*, in *Public Affairs: From Beuys to Zittel*, Kunsthaus Zürich, 2002.

Rita (built in 2005 at Tensta Konsthall, Sweden) not only draws more quickly and reliably than Hektor, but it can also erase and undo what it has just created by switching its drawing tool from white-board markers to sponges. From the production of imagery, the focus shifts to its endless reproduction and change; the act of drawing turns into a slow display technology.

Viktor (2006) took the original idea behind Hektor (of working with triangulation through four motors) and made it a reality. The respective characters of these drawing machines derive from their mark-making medium of choice, and by the situations evoked by watching them in action.

With four motors, Viktor can theoretically work at a much larger scale (up to 20m × 20m or 65ft × 65ft) on whole walls or buildings. But it took years to achieve exactly the right calibration and algorithms to provide the precision and tension in the cables at any location and motion across the wall. By that point, I had lost interest in the medium of spray paint, which has so much attached cultural meaning – you are put in the Street Art context, which never was my focus. So I looked for the opposite: something ephemeral like chalk. Equipped with a new tool-holder, Viktor can hold sticks of chalk and apply just enough pressure to leave marks on a wall covered in blackboard paint – evoking school classroom lectures.

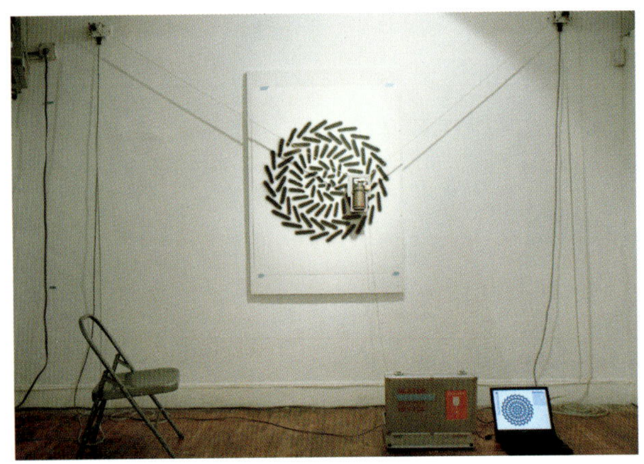

12-14 Laurenz Brunner and Jürg Lehni, *Hektor Circles* at The Artist Network, New York, 2007.

15-16 Guy Meldem with Rita, Jürg Lehni, *I'm Afraid, Dave, I'm Afraid,* at *Rita + Hektor*, Tensta Konsthall, Stockholm, 2005.

DC motors, linear bearings, semi-opaque glass, custom made tool head, controller, Scriptographer software.

17 Opposite page: detail of custom made tool head.

Central to these machines is the importance of writing, and communicating through technology. This then also became increasingly the focus of the works realized through them, in drawings that often take on the form of non-verbal lectures: a layering of topics, stories and riddles made manifest through a collage of visual references and anecdotes.

In 2008, I collaborated with Alex Rich on *A Recent History of Writing and Drawing*, an exhibition curated by Emily King at the Institute of Contemporary Arts, London. The exhibition was informed by our shared archive of the same name, a collection of source material and inspirations compiled while developing and working with the drawing machines – a history of solutions to communication problems, each one made redundant by the next, and eventually forgotten. The result is an alternative history of design and art organized in terms of tools, processes and inventions, rather than people, currents and styles. Every Thursday during the show, Viktor's actions accompanied guest artists, designers, musicians and entrepreneurs as they talked, from their various perspectives, about the creative misuse of technology.

My machines are essentially platforms for the creation of further works; there is a correspondence between their characters and the topics explored through them. As amalgams of industrial and manufactured components, the stories they tell are, similarly, collages of shared messages produced in an ongoing dialogue with different collaborators and in different scenarios.

A machine that executes a work of undeclared origin on a wall; a handheld printer that's moved like a pen and print lines of dot-matrix text; an image-and-text archive that's used to produce new work – in each case, there's a blurring of authorship. These works are less about the 'I' and more about the 'We' – to quote (loosely) Lawrence Weiner – driven by a desire to communicate openness towards their means of production, and a collective celebration of their and our existence. They speak of the human urge to communicate and share, and to live with and constantly renegotiate our relationship to technology.

16. Jürg Lehni, Viktor, 2006, close-up of chalk-head. DC motors, tool head, sprung steel coils, brushed stainless steel enclosures, cables, Scriptographer software. Viktor was supported by the Swiss Federal Office of Culture and Migros Cultural Percentage.

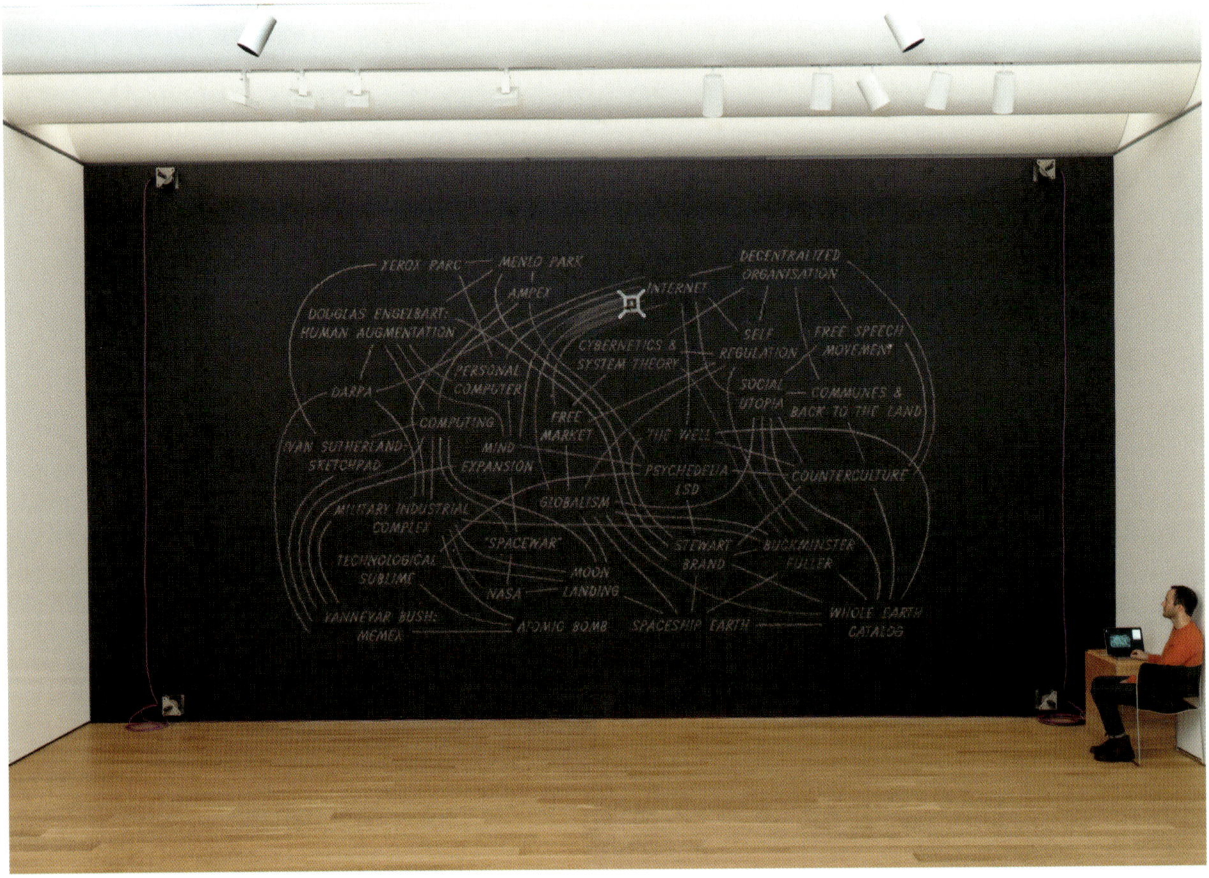

17. Jürg Lehni & Wilm Thoben drawn by Viktor, *Two Legacies* presented at Acquisition Meeting, SFMOMA Collection Center, San Francisco, 2014.

18, 19 Viktor draws chairs to accompany Michael Marriott's lecture on "A history of chairs based on technological advancements (since 3,000 BC)" as part of *A Recent History of Writing and Drawing* by Jürg Lehni and Alex Rich, ICA, London, 2008.

WWW Drawing Symposium Roundtable

WWW Drawing Symposium Roundtable

Mehrdad Hadighi

Mehrdad Hadighi: There are two things that reappeared in many presentations. The first one was ambiguity – the relationship between what one thinks is in one's head and what one sees in the material world. You have an idea; you draw something, either by hand or by computation; and you work through a series of ambiguities to make things more and more precise. You start with the least precise and gradually – at least, in architecture – you make things more and more precise until it's constructible. It's an interesting topic, certainly in relationship to computation.

The second thing is the underlying structure of the work. It was really a light-bulb moment for me when Daniel mentioned the notion of a structure which isn't the graphic structure that exists within, for example, a pencil drawing, but is independent from that. A few have argued that Jackson Pollock's work is completely structured and structural, but it's a structure of the mark, a structure that's visible in the graphic.

Janet Abrams

Janet Abrams: Let's hear the responses of James, Mark and Mike to what we've heard today and seen in the video of the WWW Drawing Workshop.

James Wines: I'm always concerned by the investment in any one medium at the expense of ideas. There are two major mistakes that are made in the arts. At my age, one assumes that one's "been there, done that, and seen everything" – and ***one hasn't***. There's always some new surprise. At the other extreme is the naiveté of youth. I've been through about six generations of gee-whiz-tech and, until the hair on the back of my neck stands up, there's no idea.

Nam June Paik and I lived right next door to each other in SoHo, so we were always conversing. We both considered our professions – architecture in my case, video technology in his – as subject matter. Most people just used the medium of video to show pictures. He used the whole medium and transformed it. When I see ideas like that emerging – we saw some of them today – I get a tingle at the back of my neck.

James Wines

In my office, we'll sit down to a meeting, having just started a project and somebody says, "Have you seen this new material? And I say, "Wait a minute. We don't even know what we're ***doing***. It could have nothing to do with new technology." We just finished a couple of projects that we could not possibly have done physically, in our digital age. But everything I did in the beginning was hand sketches with blobs of ink and trial and error.

The biggest mistake that can be made in the digital age is to throw out the baby with the bathwater. Anybody who just does digital technology is short-changing him or herself tremendously without knowing how to draw. Because you miss the area of subliminal accident and you submit yourself to a very prescriptive form of drawing that's all digitized, all gridded, all set up in advance. *Both* are very useful.

You've got to be able to do everything. You've also got to understand technology. If a building doesn't stand up, you're in deep shit, of course. So, there's the recognition of geometry, of gravity, of tradition. But the bottom line is that there's got to be an idea, something that says, "this is more than the tech, more than the media." Because the problem of architecture in particular is that it's all illustrative. I see so much architecture which is mere décor. Yes, there are the big fancy shapes, but the way it's conceived and the lack of ideas, is décor. That's a dangerous edge to walk on.

Michael Webb: I absolutely loved Jürg's presentation. Funnily enough, it made me think about ancient drawing instruments. The old ones – I sound like an old fogey now, which I am – were so much more beautiful than the newer ones. Some of them were made of mahogany, others of brass. None of you under the age of 90 knows what a ruling pen is. It's two steel blades with an ivory handle. You put ink in between the two blades, tune it with a little knob, then draw a line. Well, that carved ivory handle was so beautiful.

Left to right: Daniel Cardoso Llach, Michael Webb

I once set an assignment in a Columbia drawing class where we welded together old drawing instruments: for example, a compass attached to a pencil, attached to a pair of dividers. The shapes people started to draw were incredible: one could actually mold the paper so it became a curved shape rather than flat and that would give you a new set of shapes. Nevertheless, the instrument was always subservient to the drawing the instrument made.

In Jürg's presentation, it's exactly the opposite: the instrument is absolutely fascinating. Not only is it very elegant-looking, but to watch it move... We're floored by the beauty of this object moving. But then we look at the actual drawing it makes. I don't mean to knock you, Jürg, but that's a problem. Should it make a drawing at all? Should we just watch it *move*? Somehow, the question remains: what do you do about the *actual drawing*?

Mark West: In the late 1990s, Ursula Franklin, the Canadian thinker, scientist and cultural critic observed that today, most of our technologies are technologies not of *production*, but of *control*.[1]

In architecture, ultimately, you want as much control as possible. But in order to *find* anything, you can't be in control. Computers are machines that are controlled at every level either by their internal structure or by programming. So there's quite a constraint and chance doesn't enter in so easily.

Mark West

Then you have to get whatever's *in* the machine *out* of the machine. Eventually something has to draw something – either ink on paper or a 3D print – to get it out of the machine. Suddenly you're in this world filled with chance; no matter how much you try to control, it's also out of control – and *how* out-of-control depends on the construction tolerance of the action you're doing. There's always a version of being out of control in the full physical world.

At the heart of any discussion about any tool – especially a tool that's already so thoroughly a machine – there's another problem that has more to do with the realm of ideas. It is this: Architectural drawing *tends to produce a vision of a bloodless world*. That, to me, is really horrifying. It's something I'm ashamed of denying in my practice and something I try to find a way out of, although it's against the culture of the discipline in its current machine incarnation.

1 Ursula Franklin, *The Real World of Technology; the CBC Massey Lectures*, House of Anansi Press, 1989.

The question of control or being out-of-control – of chance, determination, holistic technologies, prescriptive technologies – all those questions are deeply related to another question which is prior to all of them: *What kind of world do we want to live in? And do our actions make our life better or not?*

Janet Abrams: Picking up on this notion of a bias towards the 'bloodless', Seher, your work is not at all separated from the blood-filled histories of the places you're actually depicting. I'm thinking particularly of the courtyards and the piece you did with the Geographical Society.

Seher Shah: Mark's idea of the architectural drawing as bloodless is quite evocative of certain individuals. But, ultimately, no matter how ambiguous or ephemeral the ideas are, essentially drawing is information that you're providing. In terms of it being bloodless, that notion just doesn't occur in my work.

Left to right: Mark West, Ann Tarantino, Seher Shah

The process is not so much about the finished drawing, but about the activity in which a drawing is made – a labour-intensive process that usually takes me one to three months; it becomes more about how one situates external and internal conditions. When I look at the courtyard, or the Royal Geographic Society's Coronation Ceremonies, or the Panorama, those drawings are conduits to get to something else. They're not just about architectural references and spaces, but about how you can shift the way information is presented. If you looked at all of us here on this panel through a photographic lens, that would be one way of being presented with a space, an environment. A plan of this arrangement would be a very different thing.

For me, drawing is more about navigating and opening up vantage points, primarily for myself, and expanding how certain historical precedents have been presented to me. Which is why I find the work of 'paper architects' so fascinating, because it's about ideology and philosophy. Somehow, in the built world, that ideology just gets bypassed. Paper architecture – because it's free of materials and scale – can do a lot more without needing the philosophy and the social circumstances. Whereas architecture and construction sometimes feel more imposed. I've been researching Brutalist architecture recently and how particular kinds of architecture and their attendant ideological facets get imposed on the landscape. Certain facets, like communal ways of living, are really beautiful. But there's a strange disconnect between what gets proposed and what gets built.

Rachel Strickland, second from right

I'm not working on construction drawings; I'm drawing in a very different mode. But the interesting thing about drawing is how you can collapse the idea of the external and historical onto internalized states and modes and questions. That never feels 'bloodless' to me. It feels expansive.

Mark West: You're talking about the state of mind when you're making drawings...

Seher Shah: A state of mind that comes with intensive labor. You don't just go in and draw a few lines (though you can, as well). It's about repetition, about the vantage points that activity opens up. 'Anxiety' seems to be a word I use a lot with 'ambiguity'. Drawing is good therapy, I guess.

Janet Abrams: I wonder whether you're still carrying over certain aspects from your training and practice as an architect, Seher. You're very disciplined in terms of the actual marks you make and your use of perspective. Some of your really big drawings are somewhat florid, which isn't typical of what we recognize as an architectural drawing, but gives the viewer something to enter. Again I'm thinking of your Royal Geographical Society project: those particular drawings and your reworked photographs seem to be taking you in a direction that more easily conveys the notion of drawing as a way of processing architectural ideologies.

Seher Shah: Drawing has this freedom: it can be whatever you want it to be. But I like parameters and architectural constraints. For example, in the case of the Coronation ceremony, I unraveled that photograph by drawing a plan and then an elevation and flattening the entire photograph. Those are very specific parameters. Within them, I have an enormous amount of room to move. I *like* the constraints. But I am conscious that the final thing is a work on paper or an object or a photograph, and there has to be a correlation throughout the whole process. It's not the sort of activity where it doesn't matter what the end-product is. That *does* matter.

Janet Abrams: Daniel, you talked about two types of technological consciousness: *Algorithmic Aesthetics* versus *Algorithmic Tectonics*. Can you pick up on the ideas Seher has just articulated, to draw parallels in the world of digital computing?

Daniel Cardoso Llach: I'll try. When I talk about technology, I'm interested in the tension between the accident and control. Sometimes, technology plays the role of the enabler of accident and serendipity and open-ended exploration. Sometimes it plays the role of an optimizing force and a controlling force – which is what Mark was referring to.

Daniel Cardoso Llach

Where I diverge is that I'm less inclined to ascribe to technology the power of full prescriptiveness. I don't think *any* technology can remove the fundamental ambiguity of the world – of our engagement with things, with our vision, with our hands. Sometimes, when we talk about technologies that are supposedly controlling, or optimizing, or in the service of a force of production, we disempower ourselves by saying "Oh, you are not free here." The same is true for vision and the way we draw with computers, write scripts, or engage with technology: *you cannot remove the fact that you are seeing what you are doing.*

And when you see what you are doing and you *act upon it* – whatever medium you are using – you are seeing in a different way every time. That is ambiguity to me. Ambiguity doesn't exist within a technology; it doesn't exist within a medium. It exists in our conversation, in the dialogue between someone, or a collective and things in the world.

Andrew Heumann: People tend to react negatively towards scripting and parametric modeling because they take the labour out of repetition and make the production of complexity and detail very automatic. It's difficult to allow for the nuance of intuitive moves during that repetitive process, because you're not producing identical repetition. In the sequential iteration of a drawing process, you can inflect it with new moves and new thoughts. One of the most beautiful ways of summing up what happens in drawing is what James refers to as the "subliminal accident."

Andrew Heumann

But accidents that occur from a scripted process – like in a Casey Reas drawing –

are accidents *after the fact*, as opposed to an accident that occurs on the subliminal level: one that occurs *as you're doing it*, and causes something to flip in the way you're operating. There are ways to engage with that in an evolution of a scripted routine or when you're directly modeling something. But there's something about those moments when you're deep in the meditation of creation and your understanding changes, and you have a feeling that guides you to a new decision you wouldn't have achieved otherwise.

Seher Shah: I actually don't think there's anything meditative about repetition. That's the opposite of what I think. I think it's all about overly-saturated design decisions. I'm trying to get through a book called *In Praise of Blandness*[2]. I always thought blandness was a really negative word. But almost every single object around us is almost hyper-designed. Objects are always imposing themselves on us. It's like a saturation of ideas. The best example I can think of is IKEA. It's not that we look at an object and impose certain decisions on *it*. Rather, the object imposes *itself* on *us*. The idea of repetition has nothing to do with meditation or meditative qualities. It's about the anxiety of over-production.

2 François Jullien, *In Praise of Blandness: Proceeding from Chinese Thought and Aesthetics*, MIT Press, 2004.

Mark West: It depends on your state of mind.

Seher Shah: I think there's a very direct correlation between drawing and one's internalized state of mind. You could be in a serene or meditative place, and the drawing might be an expression of that. When you're engaged in the activity of drawing, it's hard to talk about it. Language is difficult. Why do we *need* language to talk about the activity of drawing? It kind of defeats the purpose of the drawing.

Ann Tarantino, foreground

Ann Tarantino: While we're on the subject of things that are anxiety-provoking, there is something really terrifying about a huge blank canvas. Which is why, somewhere along the line, I lost interest in painting, and became more interested in making performative and time-based work. You go into a space and make the work; you do it and then it's *there*, and it's *there*, and it's *there*. You can't change it. It exists in space until it's blissfully painted over with a coat of paint.

Much of what we're talking about today is collaborations between human and machine. When you use the term 'bloodless', Mark, I think of a soulless Photoshop rendering of a space where there's nothing to see and it doesn't really tell me anything because I don't *know* how I might *exist* in that space, or how my body might relate to it.

What adds the blood back in is *evidence of the hand* and the marks. This is why Jürg's work is particularly interesting: you have this very elegant construction that could be making something perfect, and instead it's holding a piece of chalk and making all these feathery wisps. They're imperfect amid all of its perfection.

Michael Webb: The old guys and girls who do hand-drawing have *immense skill*. I'm thinking of Mark's drawings, and of Lebbeus Woods' drawings, especially. They know exactly how light falls on, say, a cylindrical surface; how light falling on an arm creates a shadow line, but then that shadow is illuminated from within because more light is bouncing off the chest back onto the arm. In the *Gioconda*, the transition from the light area on the forehead to a shadow line running down the throat is perfect, and it's incredible. Just like I've noticed in some of Mark's drawings. It would be shallow to say that the end of the age of easel painting led to a certain abandonment of skill, virtuosity and brilliance of execution. I suspect people will now say, "Well, you need a different sort of skill to do an abstract flat painting." I'd like to hear from the young people around us about skill. Where is the skill in contemporary computer drawing equivalent to what the Old Masters were able to do?

Audience: <laughter>

Daniel Cardoso Llach: The criterion seems to be: ***how do we get a computer drawing to emulate the realism of hand-drawing?*** I think that's a question we can answer very quickly. There are people who have the skills to create the perfect light radiosity algorithms and have written their own rendering engines that allow them to produce fantastically evocative images. But it's still a trick question, because I don't think that's the end of it.

James Wines: In visual art there's a kind of liberty whereby a drawing can stand by itself, or be a preparatory element, but it can also be an independent thing. If you look at the drawings da Vinci or Michelangelo made for architecture, versus the ones they did as drawings-unto-themselves, there's a difference in intent and content. In architecture, you're bogged down by having to ***describe*** something, but this is part of the judgemental framework by which you understand an architectural drawing. I look at an architectural drawing differently from how I look at a Pollock painting, but I ***understand*** the differences – what art is about versus what architecture is about.

Left to right: Daniel Cardoso Llach, Michael Webb, Jürg Lehni

Does an architectural drawing ***only*** have to be descriptive? No. It's on multiple other levels, particularly at the preparatory stages.

A lot of artists just do décor. Architects regard those artists as irresponsible hippies running around doing strange things. There's a weird division that didn't exist, historically. Throughout the Renaissance, you hung up your shingle as an artist; wrote poetry and sonnets; did set design, architecture, painting and sculpture. You just hung up your shingle and these activities blended together much more effectively. Nowadays we have a real problem in that issue.

Janet Abrams: Talking of hanging up one's shingle, what are the skills and tools that you could hang out on your shingle today? What software programs and languages do you have to be fluent in?

Jürg Lehni: I don't think the skill lies in mastering any particular software nowadays. Of course, it *can*, if you're following a very clear job description, and need to be able to model in Rhino or whatever.

Left to right: Michael Webb, Jürg Lehni, Mark West

But most of the time, the art lies more in mastering the medium beyond any particular software. Personally, I'm interested in computer programming as a medium. Though to me, the further down you get in terms of the layers of abstraction — the closer to the machine — the less inspiring it is.

But there's a funny moment where scripting languages come in, when it gets extremely inspiring. It's hard to explain and I constantly struggle because I can't actually talk about this stuff. But there's a level of expressiveness with some of the recent programming languages that's really mind-blowing. You can build, construct and program in a certain way. When I'm working in this way, my mindset is very close to that of an artist: I don't feel *limited* by the machines, but *liberated* by the amount of expressiveness. I'm talking about languages like Python or Ruby that have constructs like *closures* – for those who program. Whereas, when I'm programming in Java, I feel like I'm trapped in some bureaucracy, as if some bookkeeper designed the software. There are all these different 'flavors' of technology. And there are always limitations but, as artists, we *want* them.

The other interesting thing is the element of chance. When you're physically or manually working and you encounter chance as an artist, you have to recognize its potential. You might not even see it. Whereas, in the computer world – which is about control, systems that execute themselves, or parameters formulated to create automatic processes – that element of chance doesn't happen the same way. But it still happens when I see it execute. I think: "Oh, I could use it like *this*" or "I didn't think of it *that way*." I make something, it surprises me, and it takes me on a new journey.

Where I think chance is misguided is in the use of the Run function, which is basically one function code. It's not even *real* randomness, as a real computer scientist could explain to you. I get really upset when I see artworks that use randomness as a way of producing fake depth or fake complexity, because I feel that's actually cheating. There's almost a romantic idea of the machine as the artist that makes the work. You're formulating the process, and it performs its thing. I'm not interested in that at all.

Alex Terzich, left

Janet Abrams: I want to introduce Alex Terzich from the audience, because I'm sure he's got a pithy question.

Alex Terzich: I'm throwing this out from the point of view of a practitioner, someone who's in the office every day as an architect. Andrew, you introduced Daniel Libeskind's work. His *Micromegas Drawings* are real touchstones for this conversation, because they have a spatial ambiguity that everybody finds so compelling. I've always found Libeskind's built work doesn't live up to the promise of his drawings. Isn't there always a danger that the drawing holds up a promise we can never achieve, as practitioners, if it deviates too far from the realities of Cartesian grids and spatial logic?

Andrew Heumann: This connects to what we were discussing about the aesthetics of code: just because the algorithm that was involved in the design process is, in itself, inherently beautiful, doesn't mean there's any relationship between that and the production of a quality building. Any more so than the fact that the pencil drawings of Brutalist buildings had some positive intentions meant that they evolved into quality buildings.

Jane Nisselson, second from left

Jane Nisselson: I think there's something in common to both. With any truly great programmer or visualizer, their skill lies in making an idea clearer to people in a new way. It requires huge skill and insight about how to express something clearly.

Seher Shah: I want to comment on Jürg's contention that the closer you get to the machine, the less inspired you are, and that when you're in a more intuitive state, it becomes really exciting. I think that would take a remarkable amount of skill, because whatever little knowledge I have about drawing, it's a different kind of context. To relate one skill or one context to another, seems so strange. Alex, the *Micromegas Drawings* ask certain aesthetic and spatial questions, but the context in which they were conceived is very different from Libeskind's built environment. When you actually *build* that kind thing, it's a completely different context.

To equate Leonardo's shadow, chiaroscuro and certain other knowledge-based skills to computational design and code is like comparing apples and oranges. They're different skills, which can occur simultaneously in parallel, but also be unique and autonomous.

Mark West: Jürg, when you said "I can't talk about this" – that's when you enter the realm of unknowing, where many things can happen. You can wander and find things. You might ask yourself "How did I get there?" and you say can't say.

Left to right: Jürg Lehni, Mark West Ann Tarantino

When things become more refined, or more prescriptive, that magic experience disappears. The sense of unknowing is absolutely crucial. I was talking to David Wilson, of the Museum of Jurassic Technology in Los Angeles, about how wonderful and fun the Internet is. And he said, "Yes, but we're losing our sense of unknowing."

If I said, "What's the population of Norway?" no one in this room would know, but we all feel that we *could* know, because we could just look it up on Google. We have access to it somehow. So the whole atmosphere of *unknowing* – the state of mind it puts you in and the openness – there's something important about that level of complexity.

Regarding the skill question, I do think contemporary software offers users incredible power. Whether they're using SketchUp or Rhino or whatever, someone without skill can make a compelling image. When my daughter was ten years old she was making movies. That's pretty amazing, right? These tools empower people in certain ways. Of course, there's a limitation that comes with this: she can make a movie at ten, but how good is that movie going to be?

Suzanne Wines: I'm Suzanne Wines, James Wines' daughter, and I'm also an architect and educator. Michael and I shared an office at Cooper Union for years. My question goes back to Michael's original question, namely: "Now we have all this great technology, what do we do with it?" I can't tell because I straddle the generations, though I'm probably closer to my father's generation in many ways than my students' generation.

Suzanne Wines

At the turn of the 20th century, with the emergence of film and photography, there was a perception that everything had changed, which translated into art and architecture equally. The way we saw the world completely transformed. Painting and drawing had a whole new role in society, as did architecture and how it was made. Same with the printing press.

Over the last 15 years or so, since the Internet came about, the way we interact socially and acquire information has changed. How will it ultimately transform the way we live, in terms of content, seeing the world, perception? Now that all this technology changes our interaction with everything, what could the role of drawing be? How could it be completely transformed as things were, post-photography and film?

Seher Shah: Its role is to make you ask questions about the external situation, your landscape, your environment – dialogues about a whole host of things. I think drawings are, ultimately, a way of asking questions for yourself. It's peculiar when you straddle that with the formal gallery environment, where the drawings are put up framed and the public comes and asks questions about them. That's also quite an exciting moment for the work. But ultimately it's this idea of just pencil to paper – and questioning certain things for yourself. That's its role even if it's a *digital* drawing: technology is just another tool. Whether I take a piece of charcoal or wood, graphite or a digital pen, ultimately those are just tools to go through a set of questions you pose for yourself.

James Wines: A ten-year-old kid can make a movie now, but it's not really a film. A great filmmaker can make a film sometimes with very simple means. Look at the number of films that are *not* high tech; in fact, we welcome them now. I can't stand one more techie, double vision movie. There are just as many bad Renaissance paintings as in any other period. You can go to the Pitti Palace and see thousands of terrible Renaissance paintings with all the light passing over them. I remember when computers first started, I used to be dazzled by them: *God, look how crisp and sharp and clear it is.* Well, now my eyes have become trained, and I can see shit on the screen from 50 feet away.

The audience

Audience: <laughter>

Daniel Cardoso Llach: I really object. One of things that happens with this popularization of technology is that, yes, it's easier to make simple scripts, easier to make a 3D model. But that changes the way we appreciate what we do. There's the power of surprise for a while, but inevitably the really skilled craftsmanship will show, and new forms of craftsmanship will emerge. New conceptions of design quality will emerge from the new platforms and the landscape of opportunity that becomes apparent.

Now everyone can do a movie. I mean, yes, everyone can do certain *kinds of* movies, right? But there's always going to be one or two people, or a few, who will do something really interesting with the new platform or opportunity.

The roundtable

Andrew Heumann: Readily accessible tools tend to bring people to obvious solutions. like the little sparkle that crosses the screen in iMovie effects, or the appearance of a SketchUp drawing, or Instagram filters on a photo. All these things are readily available, and they have their moment of sparkle. But the speed at which the sparkle fades is increasing.

Jürg Lehni: But that's the problem of any kind of software. It's that specific thing you buy it for. There's a devaluation of the tech because of inflation, right?

Mark West: But that's what the drafting machine does. The first time I got one, it automated technical drawings, and they really looked professional. All the drawings were like this: <*snaps fingers*> You could only do certain things with the machine, but it was incredibly powerful, opening up a precision of dimension and scale and things you can't do when you're drawing by hand. It shuts down and opens up at the same time.

My daughter's friends think her films are the best films in the world. They'll grow out of it, but while they're alive and in that incarnation, they're the best films on the planet.

Suzanne Wines: Now that a ten-year-old can make a film, what is film going to do to reinvent itself? I'm thinking of Picasso and Cubism, of course.

Ann Tarantino: I think its important that you mentioned Picasso, because there's a whole trajectory of work that he made before Cubism – incredibly masterful, very rigorous drawings of busts and statues. I don't work in a representational mode, but I couldn't do what I do if I didn't know how to draw a still life, or render a space. I teach people how to draw still life and 2-point perspectives for a living, yet it's so different from what I do when left to my own devices. But those skills are still essential. It relates to this idea of knowing and unknowing: if we think of drawing as a way of understanding the world and how things relate to one another, then it will *always* be important, no matter what other tools we acquire.

Mehrdad Hadighi: I think the answer is critical engagement. I don't want to use the word 'craft', because it's too closely tied to the question of skill. I think artists are *not* craftspeople; good architects are also *not* good craftspeople, necessarily. They have to be *at least* that, but they need to be able to move beyond that. That's where critical engagement comes in.

For every beautiful shadow of the kind Mike described, there are millions of beautiful shadows done by really, really well-skilled people that result in completely schlocky paintings. We're not talking about those today. Critical engagement necessitates a certain skill level, but it cannot stay at the skill level. That's really what Jürg was talking about.

Mark, in the *WWW Drawing* movie, you talk about seeing a Rembrandt and how, close up, it's all brush strokes. That's very much the way that you, Jürg, were describing code. You're actually seeing the way this individual worked with matter, paint, with brush, with the computer application. It really is *code*: "Do I do *this*? Do I do *that*?" The level of decision-making is so intense and complex that it's far beyond skill. You have to have the skills, but you must be able to critically engage the skill, the discipline, the history, the context. In the end, that is what generates the basic work. And it's what we talk about when we talk about Rembrandt or Lebbeus Woods, and all the people around this table.

The participants

Conclusion

Mehrdad Hadighi

The WWW Drawing project, like many, started out with a simple idea that seemed compelling: to explore drawing as a mediated discipline, whether this mediation was by the hand, the pencil, or computer code.

For architects, drawing spans the entire breadth from descriptive to exploratory. Architects generally begin projects with exploratory drawings, as a way of communicating with themselves, and clarifying ideas. These drawings are non-referential, in the context of ideas that do not yet refer to a reality external to the drawing. They end projects with a set of descriptive drawings, construction documents, that refer to a future external reality, that of the building to be built.

In this context, we saw the work of the three W's as being on the exploratory end of drawing, examining issues of expression, construction, and de-construction. We also recognized that we typically experience computational drawing as being closer to the pole of representation, because computers are more efficient at producing the descriptive drawings we call construction documents. Our aim was to affirm architectural drawing of the kind engaged by three W's and also to bring to light the exploratory nature of computational drawing.

As we delved more deeply into this project, however, we discovered that these two ends of the spectrum were almost always non-existent, that, for architects, all drawing-whether hand or computationally drawn-exists in the liminal state between exploratory and descriptive. What emerged as significant, once we paired the manually-intensive work of the three W's with the computationally-intensive work discussed by other participants in the WWW Drawing Symposium, was the role of *structure* in the context of mediation. What appeared initially as the 'mediation of technology' – be it pencil or code, eye or screen – became pronounced as the 'technology of mediation'. We confirmed that drawing is always a mediated discipline; there is no such thing as *pure* or *natural* drawing. Whether this mediation occurs through the pencil or the keyboard is not so important; rather, what matters is the *structure* that permits the critical engagement between the author and the work.

During the Drawing Center panel discussion, I mentioned an experience I had had at the Van Gogh Museum in Amsterdam, on seeing a particular painting by Vincent Van Gogh for the first time in person. From far away, the *Self-Portrait with Gray Felt Hat* of 1887 appeared as I had known it from images and reproductions. As I walked closer, the painting transformed. When I was a foot away, I suddenly recognized that there was no 'thing' depicted in the painting. The Van Gogh of the self-portrait was not there. There were no flesh colors, no contours defining the figure or the hat, only repetitive brush strokes of un-mixed paint. Beard bled into the flesh, the jacket into the background, hair into the hat, and so on. What structures the entire painting is the brush stroke, applied with the repetitive strokes of the hand, with dabs of paint picked up from the palette by the paint brush and applied to the canvas. There is no mixing of the paint either on the palette or on the canvas. The canvas is structured by the juxtaposition of strokes, giving the illusion of color and shape.

At the Drawing Center symposium, the difference between the structure of a painting such as Van Gogh's and a computational work came up for discussion. The difference described was that in Van Gogh, the structure is visual, related to the eye and body, and in computational work, the structure is invisible – it is defined by code, non-visual matter, and thus creates a new drawing 'environment' that is totally different than the traditional hand drawing.

The structure of the work, whether in the measured application of paint with exact force, or in the decisive precision of the organization of code, is conducted in the context of a circulation between ideation and materialization, between things intelligible and things sensible. The difference between the Van Gogh painting and a computationally generated drawing may be that the relationship of the hand to the brush and paint, to the pressure of the stroke, may *appear* more directly connected to the body and thus more *natural*, and the precise organization of code more remote and not natural.

We can 'see', 'sense' the mediated environment of the arm/hand/brush/paint/canvas, and therefore assume a direct connection among them all and between the body and the work; we do not 'see'or 'sense' the more remote mediation through computation, and therefore assume a break between the structure of its ideation and the materialization of its output. Sometimes, the mediated environment appears so *natural* that we do not see it, and at other times, because we do not see the mediated environment, we assume a total disconnect from the body. However, mediation is always there, and works of art are only possible within this space. The mediation is the space that permits reflection, re-examination, re-iteration, and the criticality of work, be that space visible or invisible, be it pencil or code.

Biographies

Janet Abrams is an artist, writer, editor, and producer of conferences and conversations. She holds a BSc in Architecture from the Bartlett School of Architecture, London; a PhD in Architectural History, Theory and Criticism from Princeton University (1989) where she was a Fulbright Scholar; and an MFA in Ceramics from Cranbrook Academy of Art (2010). Over the past twenty years, she has addressed the shift from analog to digital in the spheres of play, mapping, and now drawing. She edited *If/Then: Play — Design Implications of New Media* (1998) at the Netherlands Design Institute, and co-edited *Else/Where: Mapping — New Cartographies of Networks and Territories* (2006) with Peter Hall, while Director of the University of Minnesota Design Institute. Janet's critical essays on art, architecture and design have appeared in publications including *Blueprint, Domus, CFile, Ceramic Review, frieze, I.D. Magazine, The Independent* and *The New York Times,* and in books including *Julie Snow: Architect* and *Profile: Pentagram Design.* Her collected portraits of architects and designers, *Daddy Wouldn't Buy Me A Bauhaus,* will be published by Princeton Architectural Press in 2020. A sculptor working primarily in ceramics and metals, she won SITE Santa Fe's 2014 SPREAD 5.0 competition for studio artists, and has had residencies at A.I.R. Vallauris, the Banff Centre, the European Ceramic Work Centre, and the MacDowell Colony.

Daniel Cardoso Llach is Assistant Professor at Carnegie Mellon University, where he teaches architecture, directs the Master of Science in Computational Design, and co-directs the Code Lab, a multidisciplinary teaching and learning laboratory focusing on creating critically informed design technologies and technically informed design criticism. His recent work includes the book *Builders of the Vision: Software and the Imagination of Design* (Routledge, 2015), which identifies and documents the theories of design emerging from postwar technology projects at MIT, and traces critically their architectural repercussions. He is a Graham Foundation grantee and his writings have been published in journals including *Design Issues*, *Architectural Research Quarterly (ARQ)*, and *Thresholds*, among others, and in several edited collections, including *The Active Image: Architecture and Engineering in the Age of Modeling* (Springer, 2017), and *DigitalSTS: A Handbook and a Fieldguide* (Princeton University Press, 2019). Daniel frequently lectures and teaches workshops around the world. He holds a Bachelor of Architecture from Universidad de los Andes, Bogotá, and a PhD and MS (with honors) in Design and Computation from MIT. He has also been a research fellow at Leuphana (MECS), Germany, and a visiting scholar at the University of Cambridge, UK.

Mehrdad Hadighi is Professor and Head of the Department of Architecture at Pennsylvania State University and Stuckeman Chair of Integrative Design. He completed his post-professional graduate studies at Cornell University and holds a professional degree in architecture and a degree in studio art from the University of Maryland. A licensed architect and founding principal of the Studio for Architecture, his premiated collaborative design competition entries include the Studentenheim + Bauernmarkt, Glockengasse, Public Space in the New American City, Atlanta, Berlin Alexanderplatz Design Competition, Austrian Cultural Institute in Manhattan, and the Peace Garden Design Competition. Hadighi was selected as one of "25 most intriguing, innovative and intrepid architects, from all over the world" by *Wallpaper** magazine in 2004 and as one of "10 Young Firms Reshaping the Globe" by *Architectural Record* in its 2003 Design Vanguard issue. His work is the subject of a monograph published by Actar (2019) and another published by SHARESTAN (2008). His recent work has been featured in books including *Conversions*; *Small Structures, Green Architecture*; *Xs Green: Big Ideas, Small Buildings*; *Extensions and Renovations*; *Up, Down, Across: Domestic Extensions*; *House Plus, New House Design*; and *Architecture In Detail.* His scholarly work focuses on drawing parallels between 20th century art, critical theory, and the constructive principles of architecture.

Andrew Heumann is an artist, technologist, and architectural designer based in New York City. As a senior researcher at WeWork, he develops new software tools and workflows for design and architecture teams. Formerly a design technology specialist at Woods Bagot and at NBBJ, he has written more than 20 plug-ins for 3D-modeling software (*Human* – the most popular – has had over 50,000 downloads) and created many bespoke tools for design teams and practices that aid in the management of project metrics, environmental and urban analysis, and façade design. Outside of his professional work, Andrew is a generative artist, working with data, algorithms, geometry, and pixels to create rich visual abstractions that engage and challenge the limits and affordances of digital media. Andrew has studied both architecture and computer science, and has lectured and taught seminars at Cornell University, Yale University, Columbia GSAPP, and the California College of the Arts. His work has been published in *Wallpaper** magazine, the *International Journal of Architectural Computing*, and *CLOG* journal, and presented at conferences including ACADIA, SIMAUD, Autodesk University, and the AEC Technology Symposium.

Jürg Lehni works collaboratively across disciplines, dealing with the nuances of technology, tools, and the human condition. His works often take the form of platforms and scenarios for production and research, such as the drawing machines Hektor, Rita, and Viktor, created to visually examine the multifaceted relationships between computer assisted creative work, mechanical reproduction and the poetic potential of mechanical gestures. He also produces software-based structures and frameworks, including *Paperjs.org*, *Scriptographer.org* and *Vectorama.org*, platforms designed to combine and explore computational and manual ways of working with graphical form and expression. Lehni has shown work internationally in group and solo shows at MoMA New York, SFMOMA, Walker Art Center, Centre Pompidou, Kunsthalle St. Gallen, Institute of Contemporary Arts London, and the Design Museum London. In 2015, his work Viktor was acquired by SFMOMA for its collection. After years of working and teaching abroad, he now runs his own studio practice in Zürich. He previously was an Associate Professor of Interaction Design at the Parsons School of Design in New York in 2016-2017; Visiting Professor at the UCLA Department of Design and Media Arts in 2012-2013; and Visiting Professor at the Academy of Fine Arts, Nuremberg, in 2015.

Jane Nisselson is a film director and associate multimedia director at the School of Engineering and Applied Science at Columbia University, New York. Through her films, Jane reveals different kinds of systems — of scientific models, innovation, diagrams, molecules, design strategies, and fragrances. A graduate of the MIT Media Lab, she worked at the New York Institute of Technology as a software developer and animator before opening her New York-based media company, Virtual Beauty, which produced Webby-nominated short documentaries for clients including Condé Nast, Corning Museum of Glass, International Flavors & Fragrances, MoMA, The New School, Popular Mechanics, University of Minnesota Design Institute, *W Magazine* and the Wyss Institute at Harvard University. Nisselson's grant-based projects include a National Science Foundation funded video titled *Explaining Diagrams* and a resident scholarship to film molecular models built by Linus Pauling. She teaches a workshop on modular filmmaking at the New School and has lectured at SIGGRAPH, Verge NYC, the SVA Design Research program, and the MIT School of Architecture.

Seher Shah works between the fields of art and architecture. She evokes both these traditions of drawing in her artistic practice, using a personal and rigorous formalism to trouble the otherwise rational language of architectural drawing. Through her career Seher has used a formal approach for different lines of inquiry: she has investigated how architectural fragments can capture and retain meanings and memories and how they can be reconfigured to represent complex subjectivities; she has examined the relationship, in terms of both form and scale, of architectural structures and their surrounding landscapes; and she has delved into the rich history and legacy of modernist architecture through drawing, sculpture and printmaking. Her work has been exhibited at several international institutions including The Museum of Modern Art, Centre Pompidou, Nasher Museum of Art, Victoria and Albert Museum, House of World Cultures, Austin Museum of Art, Queens Museum of Art, Brooklyn Museum, The Drawing Room, Kiran Nader Museum of Art, Momenta Art and Exit Art amongst others. Born in 1975 in Karachi, Pakistan, Seher grew up in London, Brussels and New York City. She received her Bachelor of Fine Arts and Bachelor of Architecture from the Rhode Island School of Design in 1998.

Ann Tarantino is an artist working across drawing, painting, installation, and site-specific works of public art. Her work has been exhibited widely in the US and overseas, and has appeared in settings ranging from museums and galleries to botanical gardens and city streets. Recent exhibitions and projects include *Cloud Countries*, a new installation created for the Pittsburgh International Airport (2018); *Watermark*, a major public commission for the community of Millvale, PA; and *Razzle Dazzle*, a 400-foot-long painting installation running beneath the Brooklyn Bridge, commissioned by the New York City Metropolitan Transit Authority. She was featured in *New American Paintings* in 2005 and 2007, and was a 2016-17 recipient of a Fulbright Core Scholar Award for artistic practice in Brazil; while there, she developed a new body of works on paper and panel exploring the colors and textures of the Brazilian landscape during several months in São Paulo and Belo Horizonte. Ann earned an honors degree in Visual Arts from Brown University in 1997 and a Master of Fine Arts with a concentration in Painting from The Pennsylvania State University in 2001. She is Assistant Professor of Art at Penn State University, where she teaches courses in drawing, painting, and curatorial practices, and directs and curates university gallery spaces.

Michael Webb is an artist operating at the intersection of art and architecture. Born at Henley on Thames, England, in 1937, he trained in architecture at the Regent Street Polytechnic School of Architecture (now University of Westminster). One of his student projects found its way into MoMA's 1961 *Visionary Architecture* exhibition, and his thesis project — for an entertainment center in London — was repeatedly failed but subsequently widely published. In 1963, Webb joined Archigram, often called the "Beatles of Architecture," whose work rebelled against the British architectural establishment's failure to recognize the era's dynamic social and technological changes. Archigram was awarded the 2002 RIBA Gold Medal. Michael moved to the US in 1965 to teach at Virginia Tech, and has since taught architecture at RISD, NJIT, Columbia University, Barnard College, Cooper Union, SUNY Buffalo, Pratt Institute and Princeton University. He has had solo exhibitions of his drawings and paintings (including the *Temple Island Study* and *Drive-in House* series) at Cooper Union, Columbia University, Storefront for Art and Architecture, Architecture League, University of Manitoba, and Art Net Gallery, London. He was a 2011 Senior Mellon Fellow at the CCA, Montreal.His recent monograph, *Two Journeys* (Lars Müller, 2018) features essays by Kenneth Frampton, Michael Sorkin and Mark Wigley, and nearly 200 of his drawings: artistic works rooted in analytical thinking, and structured around architectural elements and notational systems.

Mark West has taught architecture for over thirty-five years at universities in the US, Canada, and Europe, while working as an artist, inventor and independent researcher. He is the inventor of fabric-formed concrete techniques for architecture and engineering structures and the author of *The Fabric Formwork Book: Methods for Building New Architectural and Structural Forms in Concrete* (Routledge, 2016). Mark received his practical education working as a builder, and his professional architectural education at The Cooper Union. His works, as both builder and artist, merge the disciplines of drawing, sculpture, painting, architectural design, construction, and structural engineering. Most recently he has moved his work to Montreal, Canada where his speculative and practical experiments have free reign in the *Surviving Logic* atelier (www.survivinglogic.ca).

James Wines is the founder and president of SITE, an environmental art and architecture organization chartered in New York City in 1970. He is the former Chairman of Environmental Design at Parsons School of Design and a Professor of Architecture at Penn State University. His architecture, landscape, and public space projects are based on a site-specific response to surrounding contexts. Wines' educational philosophy advocates 'integrative thinking' as a means of including multi-disciplinary ideas from outside the design professions. He has written seven books on art and design, including *On Site-On Energy* (Scribners & Sons, 1974), *De-Architecture* (Rizzoli International, 1987) and *Green Architecture* (Taschen Verlag, 2000). He has designed more than 150 buildings and environmental art works for private and municipal clients in eleven countries. James received the Smithsonian Institution's 2013 National Design Award for Lifetime Achievement, the 2011 ANCE Annual Award for an International Architect (Italy), and the 1995 Chrysler Award for Design Innovation (USA). He has also received fellowships and grants from the National Endowment for the Arts, Kress Foundation, American Academy in Rome, Guggenheim Foundation, Rockefeller Foundation, Graham Foundation and Ford Foundation.

Acknowledgments

This book and the events leading up to it were made possible by the generosity and adventurous vision of H. Campbell (Cal) and Eleanor R. Stuckeman.

Nathaniel Quincy Belcher, the former Director of the Stuckeman School of Architecture and Landscape Architecture, supported the WWW Drawing project with funds from the Stuckeman Family Endowment.

The WWW Drawing project would not have come about without the inspirational drawing skills of James Wines and the late Lebbeus Woods — one of the original W's, who sadly passed away shortly after it was launched.

The Drawing Center, New York, generously hosted the WWW Drawing Symposium, enabling us to bring the dialogue to a wider audience.

We are indebted to all the participants for their efforts throughout the WWW Drawing project, and during the process of documenting it in this publication.

WWW Drawing:
Architectural Drawing from Pencil to Pixel

WWW Drawing — a project of the
Department of Architecture, Stuckeman School of Architecture
and Landscape Architecture,
College of Arts and Architecture, Pennsylvania State University

Conceived and directed by
Mehrdad Hadighi
Professor and Head of Architecture
Pennsylvania State University

Produced and book edited by
Janet Abrams

Design: Marga Gibert, Actar Publishers

Design assistance:
Connor Pritz
Mark Yeakey

WWW Drawing video documentary
a Virtual Beauty production
Jane Nisselson, Director
Rachel Strickland, Director of Photography
Cody Goddard, Camera Assistant/Sound
Eric Weiss, Time Lapse Photographer

Special Thanks to:

Michael Webb
Mark West
James Wines

Daniel Cardoso Llach
Andrew Heumann
Jürg Lehni
Seher Shah
Ann Tarantino

and

The Drawing Center, New York,
for hosting the symposium

Photography credits:
Janet Abrams: cover, pp 50-51, 52-55, 58-59, 62-67.
Tom Little: p 88.
Cody Goddard and Eric Weiss: pp 60-61 and 68-69.
Kristy Yang: Roundtable photographs, pp 112-121.

Printing and binding
Arlequin

Distribution
Actar D, Inc. New York, Barcelona.

New York
440 Park Avenue South, 17th Floor
New York, NY 10016, USA
T +1 212 966 2207
E salesnewyork@actar-d.com

Barcelona
Roca i Batlle 2-4
08023 Barcelona, Spain
T +34 933 282 183
E eurosales@actar-d.com

Indexing
English ISBN: 978-1-948765-22-0
PCN: Library of Congress Control Number: 2019934171
Publication date: 2020